The Art of Golf

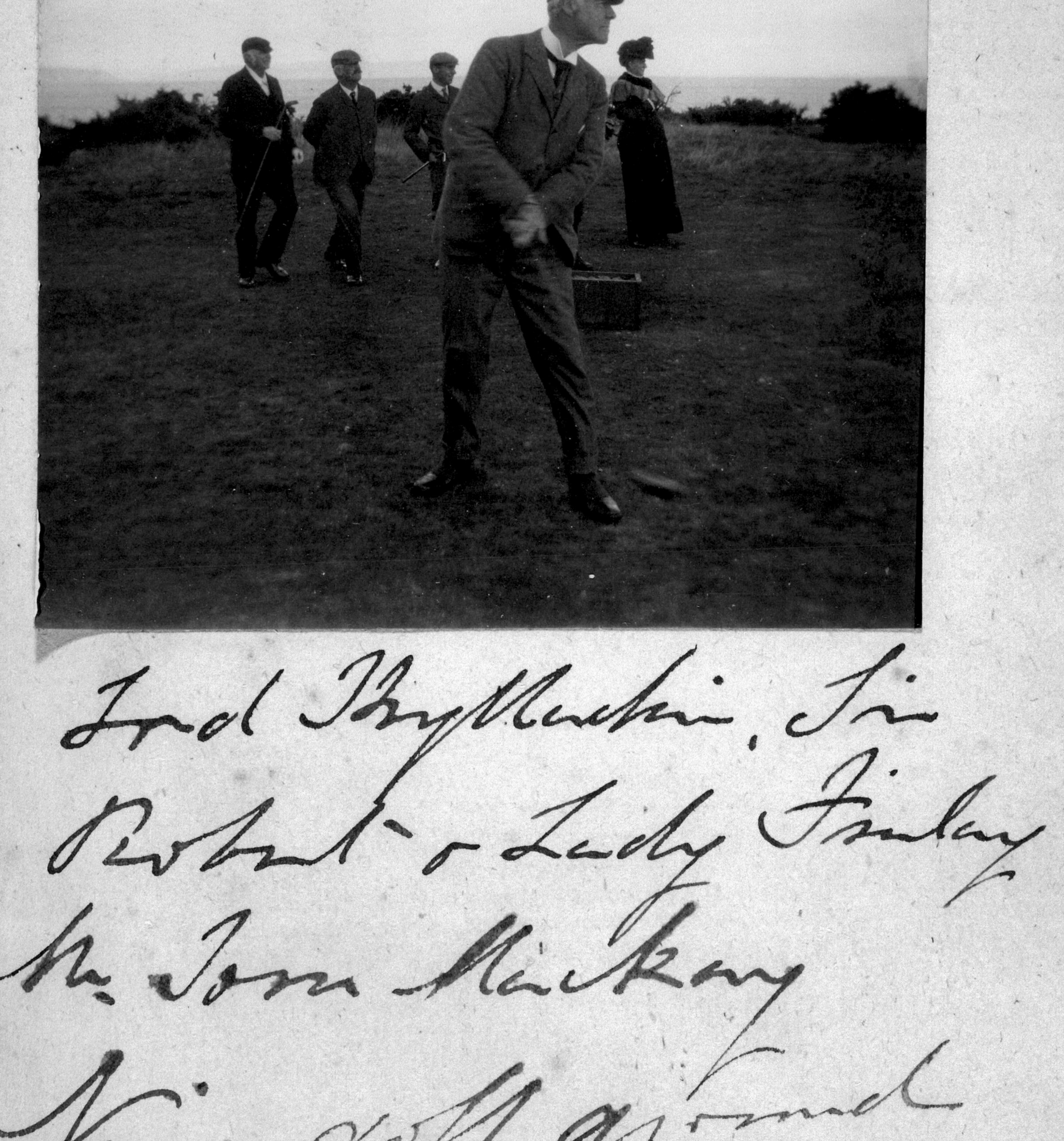

Lord Strathnairn, Sir
Robert & Lady Finlay
Mr Tom Mackay
Nairn Golf ground

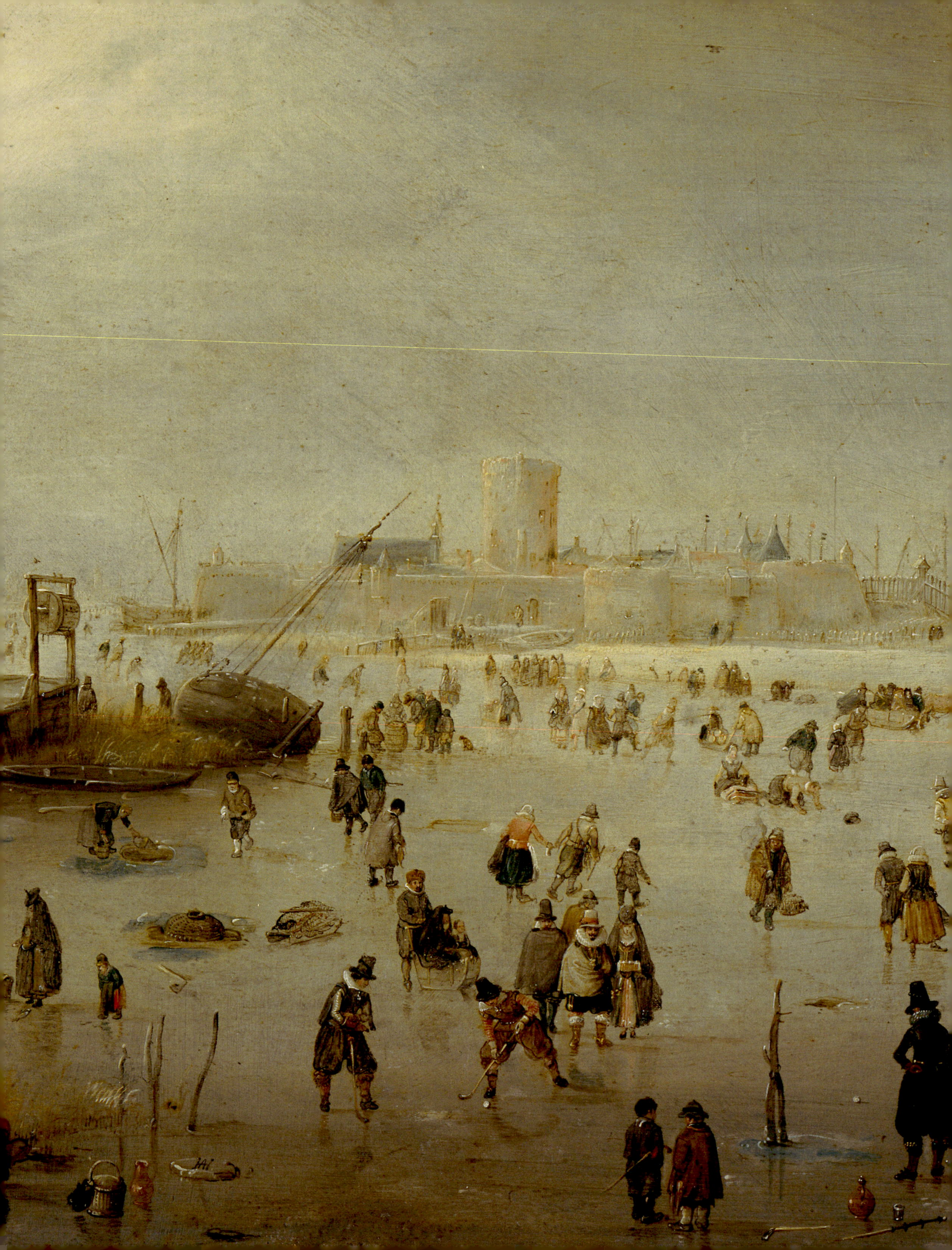

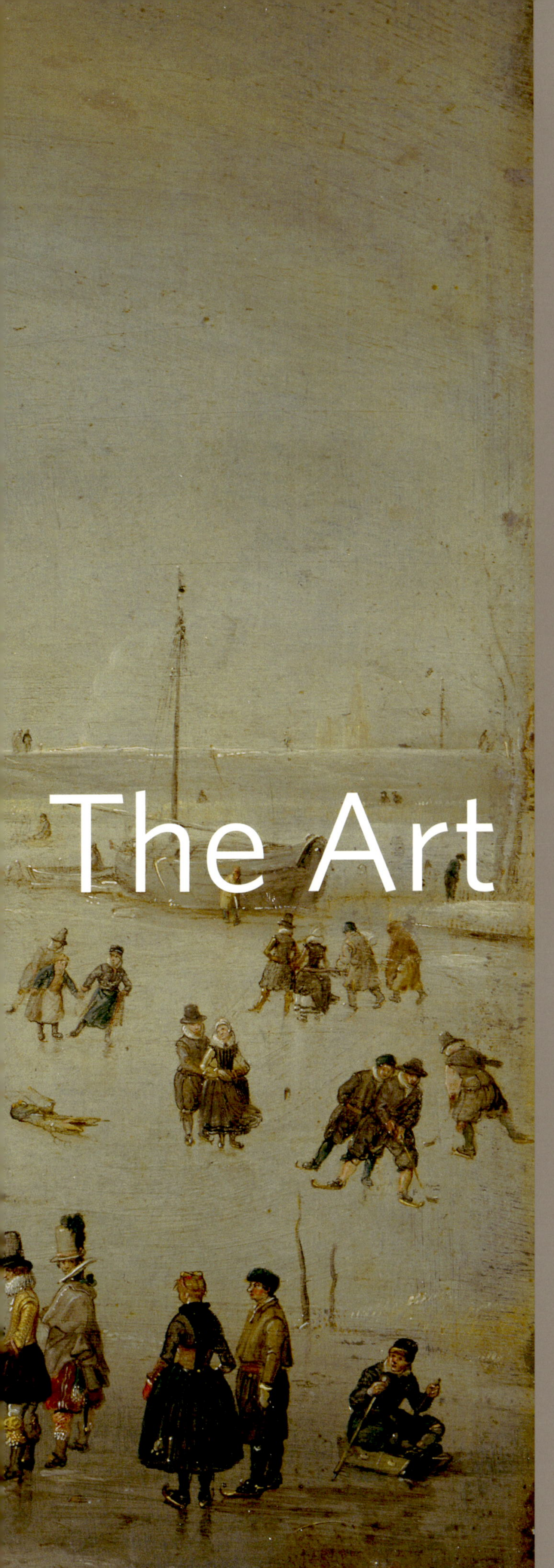

ESSAYS BY

Rand Jerris, Ph.D.

Catherine M. Lewis, Ph.D.

Richard Anthony Lewis, Ph.D.

Jordan Mearns

Christian Tico Seifert, Ph.D.

The Art of Golf

HIGH MUSEUM OF ART, ATLANTA

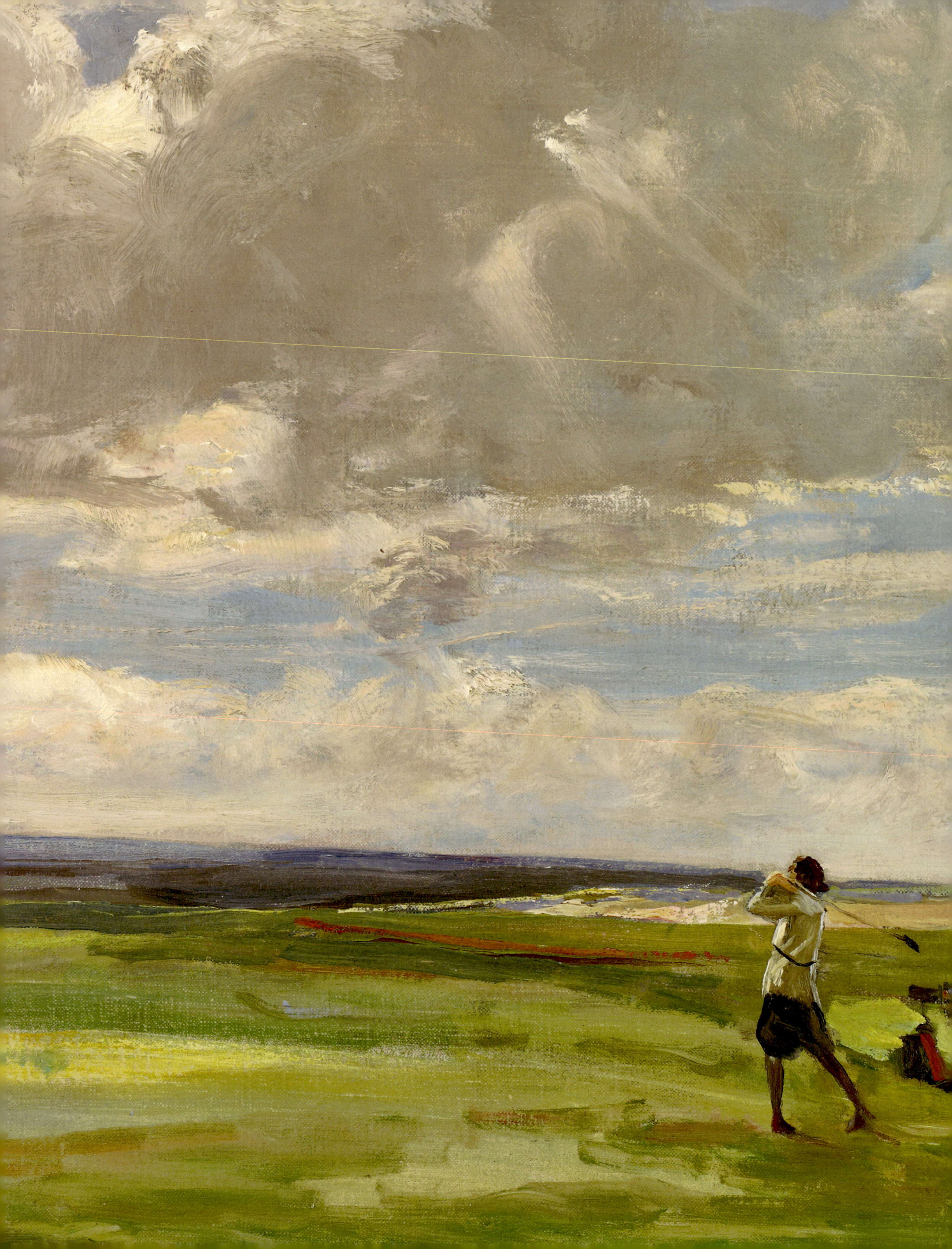

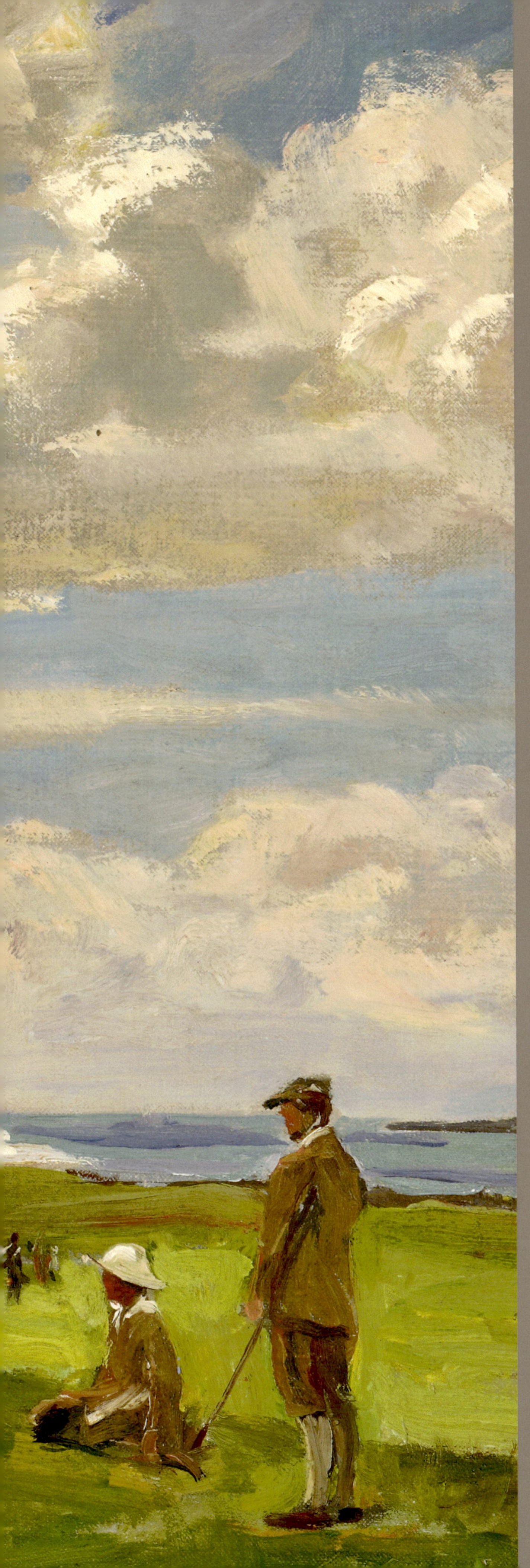

HIGH MUSEUM OF ART

The High Museum of Art recently entered into a multiyear partnership with the National Galleries of Scotland. After successfully organizing and touring *Titian and the Golden Age of Venetian Painting: Masterpieces from the National Galleries of Scotland*, John Leighton, Director-General of the National Galleries of Scotland, Michael Clarke, Director of the Scottish National Gallery, and I began to think about what would be the next collaborative project.

On a June 2009 trip to Scotland, Michael Clarke pointed out that the National Galleries of Scotland together with The Royal and Ancient Golf Club of St Andrews jointly own one of the most celebrated historical images of the game of golf, a painting by Charles Lees simply titled *The Golfers*. The painting portrays in detail a match played on the Old Course at St Andrews in 1847. This masterpiece of the Victorian era has never before traveled to the United States, though reproductions of it hang in golf clubhouses around the world—thus the core of an idea was born. We knew we would be able to tell the story of Lees's conception and execution of this famous painting, since many of his preparatory sketches still exist and are owned by the National Galleries of Scotland and The Royal and Ancient Golf Club of St Andrews, including portraits of the individuals depicted in the painting; there is even a very early photograph by Robert Adamson and David Octavius Hill—perhaps the first photographic image of golf—to which Lees referred as he composed his painting.

As we talked further, the idea of a broader exhibition on the art of golf unfolded quite naturally. Golf is an important part of the cultures of both Scotland and the United States—Scotland as the spiritual home of golf, and Georgia, particularly Atlanta, as the home of Bobby Jones, and Augusta as the home of the Masters Tournament. We began to plan an exhibition that would focus on the Charles Lees painting and the legacy of Bobby Jones. But as we dug deeper, it became clear that there was a story here that had never been told through art and that, in fact, many artists over the last four hundred years have used the sport as their subject and were inspired by the heroes of the game in both Scotland and the United States. Our research revealed that artists as varied as Rembrandt van Rijn, Sir Henry Raeburn, Sir John Lavery, Norman Rockwell, George Bellows, Childe Hassam, Harold Edgerton, and Andy Warhol all explored golf and related games as subjects.

The Art of Golf examines the game as depicted by landscape and portrait artists, photographers, and Pop artists through the ages. It is the first exhibition devoted to the game by a major American art museum. Comprising approximately ninety works, *The Art of Golf* examines the game's origins, its foundation in Scotland, and its growth in America in the twentieth century. The exhibition brings together rare and sometimes whimsical works of art, some of which have never before been on public display, into an artistic narrative. We are delighted to be exploring the intersection of sport, history, and art with our audiences, while at the same time continuing the tradition of bringing great works of art to Atlanta.

—

This book and the exhibition it accompanies would not have come to fruition without the cooperation and assistance of many individuals and institutions.

In 2010 I invited Dr. Catherine M. Lewis, professor, golf historian, and author of nine books, to serve as the consulting curator for this project. I want to thank her for her expertise, insightful catalogue essay, and energetic commitment to this project. Special thanks to all the catalogue essayists, including Dr. Christian Tico Seifert, the Scottish National Gallery's Senior Curator of Northern European Art, who expertly presented the Dutch antecedents of the game; Jordan Mearns, for his comprehensive look at the art of golf in Scotland; and Dr. Richard A. Lewis, Curator of Visual Arts, Louisiana State Museum, and Dr. Rand Jerris, Senior Managing Director of Public Services, United States Golf Association, who joined Catherine Lewis in penning the essay on golf in the United States.

I express my thanks to the individuals and corporations who have made this exhibition possible, including Lead Sponsor Sotheby's, The Imlay Foundation, The Sara Giles Moore Foundation, and the Friends of Scotland: Frances Bunzl, Marcia and John Donnell, Gayle Kennedy, Jo Ann and Nick Nicholson, Kathy and Bill Rayner, Sharon and Chip Shirley, Margaretta Taylor, Joan N. Whitcomb, and the Dorothy and Charlie Yates Family Fund. Additional support is provided by The Fay and Barrett Howell Exhibition Fund, The Eleanor McDonald Storza Exhibition Endowment Fund, Audio Visual Sponsor AVYVE, Alston & Bird, Ernst & Young, King & Spalding, Norfolk Southern, Doug Hertz, and William A. Parker, Jr.

I would like to thank John and Mary Ellen Imlay for their leadership in this project and passion for the game of golf—from lending pieces to the exhibition from their personal collection to leading our fund-raising efforts. They truly embody the Scottish-American love of the game.

Special thanks go to legendary golfer Jack Nicklaus and his team, including Scott Tolley, at Jack Nicklaus and the Nicklaus Companies for lending his passion for the game of golf as part of the introductory video, which welcomes our visitors and sets the stage for the exhibition.

The exhibition would not have been possible without the generosity and support of the High Museum's Board of Directors and its directors, including Philip Verre, Chief Operating Officer; David Brenneman, Director of Collections and Exhibitions and Frances B. Bunzl Family Curator of European Art; Susan Clark, Director of Marketing and Communications; Rhonda Matheison, Chief Financial Officer; Patricia Rodewald, Eleanor McDonald Storza Director of Education; and Kimberly Watson, Director of Museum Advancement.

I would like to acknowledge the entire staff of the High Museum, particularly Julia Forbes, our talented Shannon Landing Amos Head of Museum Interpretation, whose love of golf made her a natural choice to serve as the exhibition's managing curator; Angela Jaeger, Senior Manager of Creative Services; Rachel Bohan, Associate Editor; Woodie Wisebram, Senior Development Manager; Jody Cohen, Senior Manager of Exhibitions and Special Initiatives; Amy Simon, Manager of Exhibitions; Frances Francis, Senior Registrar; Rebecca Parker, Associate Registrar, Exhibitions; Jim Waters, Exhibitions Designer; Virginia Shearer, Associate Director of Education for Public Programs; Lisa Hooten, Head of School Programs; Cassandra Champion Streich, Senior Manager of Public Relations; Jennifer Bahus, Senior Manager of Advertising and Promotions; Meredith Ream, Manager of Special Events; Jodi O'Gara, Manager of Group Sales; Kevin Streiter, Manager of Facilities and Logistics; Sylvia Roberts, Head of Retail Operations; and Al Holland, Chief of Security. To everyone at the Museum who contributed to this important project: thank you.

Several members of the community have been champions of this exhibition and lent their expertise to help us make contacts, build awareness, and provide guidance about the game of golf. In particular, I thank John Companiotte and Jason Lutes.

I am especially grateful to the institutions and individuals who graciously agreed to lend works of art to this exhibition: John Leighton, Director-General, National Galleries of Scotland; Michael Clarke, Director, Scottish National Gallery; Angela Howe, Director, Museum and Heritage, British Golf Museum; Robert Williams, Director, United States Golf Association Museum; J. D. McClatchy, President, American Academy of Arts and Letters; Sal Cilella, President and Chief Executive Officer, Atlanta History Center; Davis Stewart, Club President, and Chris Borders, General Manager, Atlanta Athletic Club; Lawrence L. Gellerstedt III, President and Director, The Commerce Club; John Pyne, President, The Links Club; Timothy Sheehan, President, Cherokee Art Endowment Corporation of Cherokee Town & Country Club; Aaron Betsky, Director, Cincinnati Art Museum; Kaywin Feldman, Director and President, Minneapolis Institute of Arts; Elizabeth Glassman, President and Chief Executive Officer, Terra Foundation for American Art; Glenn Lowry, Director, The Museum of Modern Art; Eric C. Shiner, Director, The Andy Warhol Museum; John and Mary Ellen Imlay; the Yates Family; Naomi Yang; and *The New Yorker* magazine.

MICHAEL E. SHAPIRO
Nancy and Holcombe T. Green, Jr., Director
High Museum of Art
Atlanta, Georgia

NATIONAL GALLERIES OF SCOTLAND

Golf and art require many skills, some of them specific to one activity or the other, but some common to both, such as touch and vision. The finessing of a delicate chip or putt is every bit as finicky as a tricky piece of drawing or brushwork. Outstanding golfers display vivid powers of imagination as they conjure up a "shaped" shot to take account of the layout of the terrain and the prevailing weather conditions. The great landscape painters face similar challenges as they seek to portray areas of outstanding beauty and interest, matching their performance with brush and pencil to the shapes and wonders of the natural world spread out before them.

The noble game of golf—or "gowf," as it was once known in Scotland—has inspired great writers on both sides of the Atlantic, such as P. G. Wodehouse and John Updike. This exhibition demonstrates that golf has also inspired great artists. *The Art of Golf* represents a happy collaboration between the National Galleries of Scotland, the country that lays claim to being the "home of golf," and the High Museum of Art in Atlanta, a city rich in golfing history and forever associated with the great Bobby Jones, himself a lover and admirer of Scotland and of the famous Old Course at St Andrews, in particular.

This is the second in a series of exhibitions we are organizing with the High, the first of which was *Titian and the Golden Age of Venetian Painting: Masterpieces from the National Galleries of Scotland*, shown at the High in 2009–2010. We are deeply grateful to Michael Shapiro, Nancy and Holcombe T. Green, Jr., Director, and all his colleagues at the High for the enthusiasm and imagination with which they have embraced this project. The Atlantan Friends of Scotland have kindly given much encouragement throughout. In Scotland we have received tremendous support from The Royal and Ancient Golf Club of St Andrews and are deeply honored by their generous participation.

We shall measure the success of this show by the degree to which it brings together two great audiences, those of art and golf. The pianist and conductor Daniel Barenboim recently argued in his book *Everything Is Connected* that music can be taken as a metaphor for life and that we need to recognize our interdependency on one another. Golf, with its code of honor and its challenges, also teaches us how to conduct ourselves. This fascinating show provides a rich visual history of this wonderful game.

This is the first major international loan show on golf and art, and we are indebted to our colleagues at the High Museum of Art for ensuring that this has been such a stimulating and enjoyable collaboration. We thank Dr. David Brenneman, Director of Collections and Exhibitions, and in particular Julia Forbes, Shannon Landing Amos Head of Museum Interpretation, who has acted as in-house curator and carefully shepherded the project at every stage. She and all of her colleagues at the High have done a splendid job. Dr. Catherine M. Lewis, a noted historian of golf, the exhibition's consulting curator, and a contributor to the catalogue, has provided great expert knowledge over the course of the collaboration. For this we are very grateful.

We have been privileged to enjoy the unstinting support of The Royal and Ancient Golf Club of St Andrews, and we thank its chief executive, Peter Dawson; his fellow directors; Air Chief Marshal Sir Patrick Hine, Captain of the Club; and the Club Committee for the generous loans they have made to the exhibition. At the British Golf Museum at St Andrews, Director Angela Howe has been a wonderful source of support and advice throughout the planning of the show, while Peter Lewis graciously provided video footage to be used in the exhibition. Sir Michael Bonallack, one of Britain's greatest amateur golfers and a past secretary and captain of the Club, has kindly recorded an interview for the introductory video.

At the Scottish National Gallery we acknowledge with gratitude all the sterling work undertaken by Jordan Mearns, a Ph.D. candidate in the History of Art at the University of Edinburgh, who was engaged as the research assistant for the exhibition, undertook much of its administration in Scotland, and has contributed to the catalogue an essay on the history of golf in Scotland. Dr. Christian Tico Seifert, Senior Curator of Northern European Art, Scottish National Gallery, has kindly contributed a short essay on *kolf* and Dutch art. At our neighboring institution, the National Library of Scotland, Olive Geddes has provided expert help and advice.

Lenders have responded with great generosity to our many requests. We are indebted to them all, with a special mention for Archie Baird and his distinguished collection of golfing art. A number of prestigious clubs have assisted us in various ways: Royal Aberdeen Golf Club, North Berwick Golf Club, Crail Golfing Society, Elie Golf Club, Gleneagles,

Kingsbarns Golf Links, and the Honourable Company of Edinburgh Golfers at Muirfield.
Francesca Risino kindly acted as our driver on our many excursions.

On a personal level, John and Mary Ellen Imlay deserve thanks for their hospitality and
support on both sides of the Atlantic. The artist Hugh Dodd has not only lent his own work
to the exhibition but has provided fine company on the links as well. Keen golfers and
High Museum supporters Sharon and Chip Shirley have patiently watched Michael Clarke
dispatch that little white ball to all four corners as their friendship miraculously endured.

JOHN LEIGHTON
Director-General, National Galleries of Scotland

MICHAEL CLARKE
Director, Scottish National Gallery

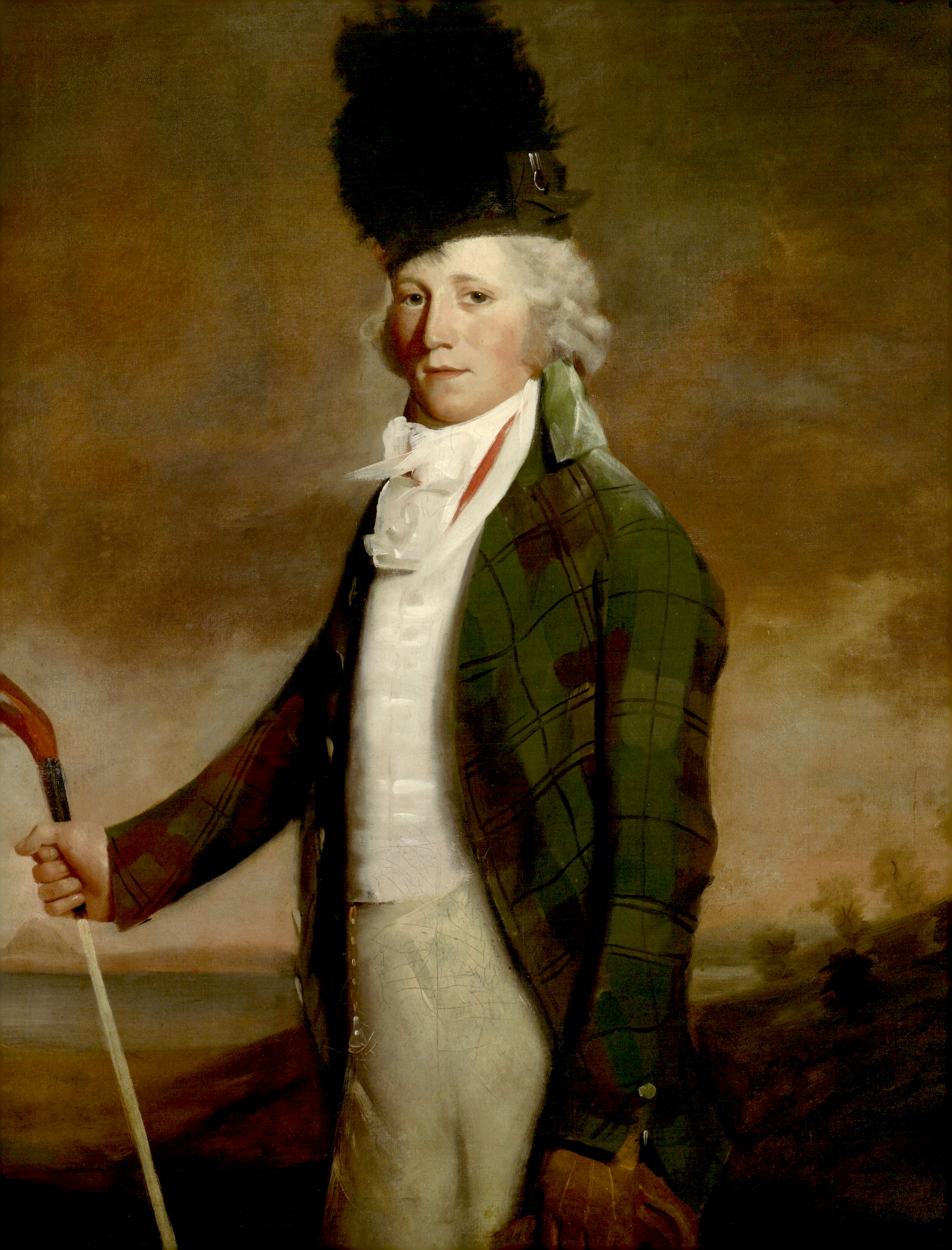

In 1992 the High Museum of Art organized the exhibition *This Sporting Life: 1878–1991*, which toured to four U.S. venues in addition to its presentation at the High. The exhibition focused on the role photographers and the technology of the camera played in capturing and disseminating moments of great drama and considered the relationship of sport to social and cultural issues. Now, almost twenty years later, the High and the National Galleries of Scotland bring together for the first time a group of paintings, illustrations, and photographs—Dutch, Scottish, and American—that illustrate how artists have used the sport of golf as a subject for numerous portraits, landscapes, and genre paintings.

Golf's origins are a source of mystery and speculation, and artists throughout the centuries have depicted games that share in its evolution. This exhibition and its accompanying catalogue begin by tackling how the Dutch game called *kolf*, which is played on ice, relates to the game of golf and the role Scotland played in the development of the modern game. Dutch artists of the seventeenth century, including Rembrandt van Rijn, Hendrick Avercamp, and Paul Bril, painted joyous winter scenes filled with people playing a variety of games on the ice or on expansive landscapes. Players—usually men—were equipped with long sticks and balls and played in pairs, aiming at a target, possibly a tree stump. While the modern game of golf that developed in Scotland is quite different from the games played in the Netherlands, many historians believe that active trade between the two nations helped influence the game of golf we play today.

There is a long tradition and an extensive body of literature devoted to the study of the history of golf, but little on its artistic representation. Golf historians, most of whom are golfers themselves, have produced exhaustive works that cover all aspects of the history of the game—from the early history to the complex rules that govern play. The art of golf, on the other hand, has been little examined, especially in comparison to other types of sporting art, such as scenes of horse racing, hunting, and boxing.

Golf in Scotland in the eighteenth century, arguably the game's formative era, is also the period in which it first inspired Scottish artists, many of whom were avid competitors. Grand portraits represent kilt-clad members of the great Scottish golf clubs equipped with club and ball. By the mid-nineteenth century—to which belong two of golfing art's masterpieces, Sir Francis Grant's *Golf at North Berwick* and Charles Lees's *The Golfers*—

artists had turned to a more representational approach, showing golfers on the links in verdant landscapes, while early twentieth-century paintings of the game are imbued with an air of elegance. Golf's popularity had spread beyond the British Isles, and its international appeal was confirmed. Golfing scenes by Sir John Lavery illustrate the importance of the game to the Scottish elite, while Art Deco railway posters advertised Scotland's premier courses to an expanding leisure class in Britain. Bringing the exhibition into the twenty-first century, newly commissioned aerial photographs by Patricia Macdonald capture the beauty of Scottish golf courses, including the Old Course at St Andrews and other great seaside courses ("links"), and the stunning inland golf complex of Gleneagles, located in majestic Perthshire, "gateway" to the Highlands.

Golf was popularized in America by such notable figures as Atlanta native Robert Tyre "Bobby" Jones, Jr. (1902–1971). As the only golfer in history to win the Grand Slam, he left an enduring legacy that extends to the building of the Augusta National Golf Club and the Masters Tournament. Jones served as an important ambassador to the golfing world, building a lasting bridge between the United States and Scotland that *The Art of Golf* celebrates. Many artists were fascinated by Jones and the amateur sporting ideal he came to represent; this exhibition includes portraits by Wayman Adams and John A. A. Berrie, among others.

Other artists drawn to golf as a subject include Childe Hassam, George Bellows, James McNeill Whistler, Norman Rockwell, and even Andy Warhol, whose iconic screenprint of golf superstar Jack Nicklaus was part of his *Athlete Series*, a group of ten paintings of the greatest sports figures of the day. Photographers have also found golf an enduring subject, and here we showcase the haunting black-and-white landscapes of Chinese American photographer John Yang as well as a series of technical photographs created by Harold Edgerton, developer of stroboscopic photography, featuring Bobby Jones hitting a golf ball. Documentary photographs of notable African American golfers reflect their importance to the history of the game, as well as their widespread exclusion from it in the nineteenth century and the first half of the twentieth.

The Art of Golf is full of surprises, from Charles Lees's intimate sketches for *The Golfers* to Whistler's *Grey and Silver: The Golf Links Dublin* to Larry Rivers's portrait of Arnold Palmer.

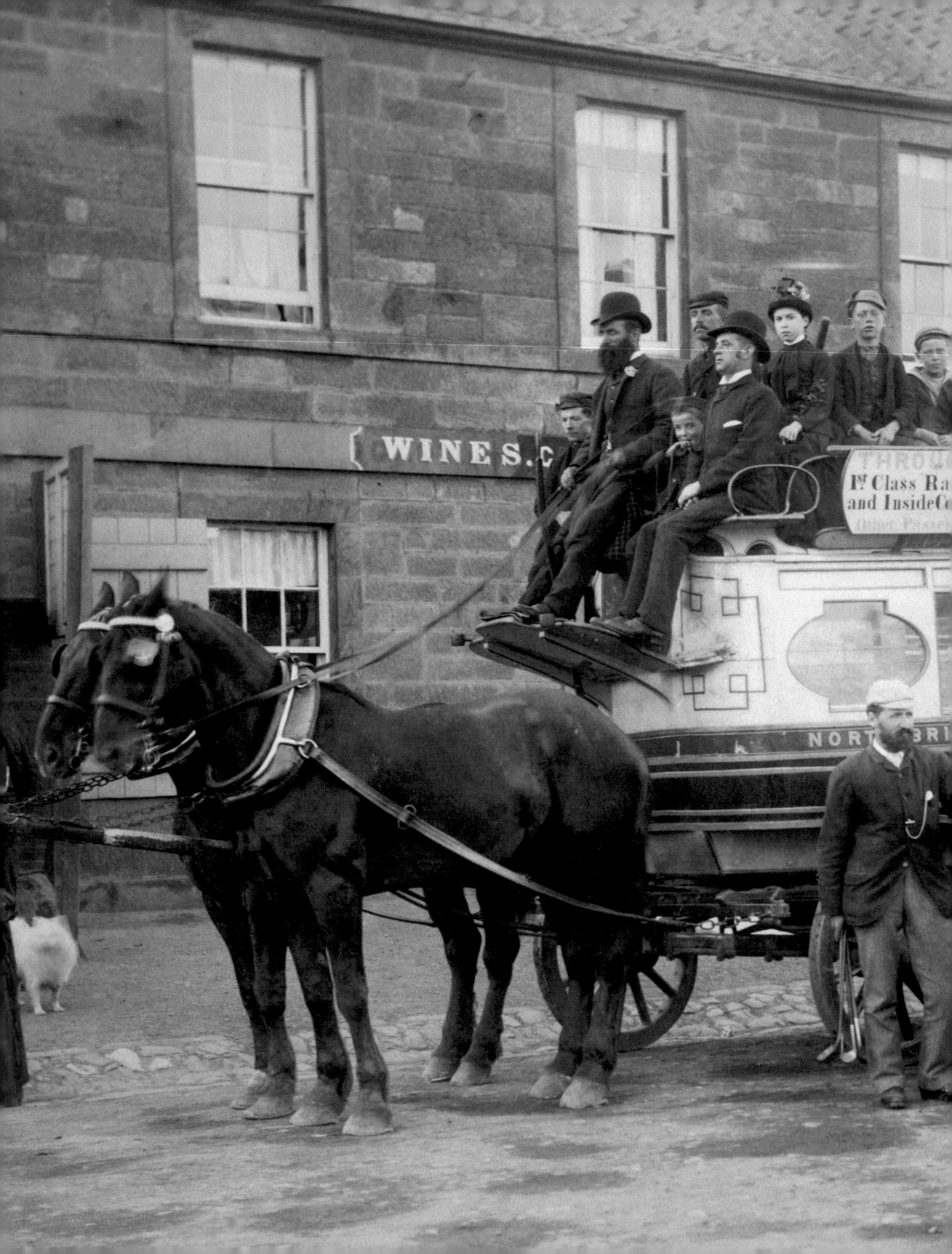

WINES.C
THROU
1st Class Ra
and InsideC
Other Passe
NORTH BRI

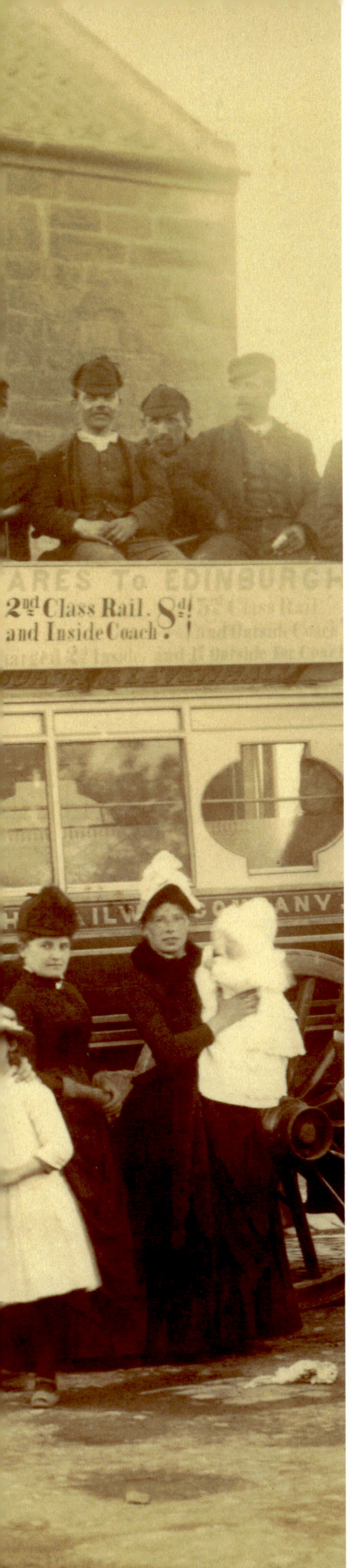

While golf is often used as a metaphor for the "Game of Life," humor is an essential part of the game. To that end, we have included cartoons from *The New Yorker* magazine and originals from Charles Schulz to represent the whimsical aspect of the game that Mark Twain once called "a good walk spoiled."

The Art of Golf has been a truly collaborative project, and many individuals assisted us on this journey. We are particularly grateful for our partnership with the National Galleries of Scotland and the great working relationship we had with Michael Clarke, Director of the Scottish National Gallery, and his research assistant Jordan Mearns. We would like to recognize Dr. Richard A. Lewis at the Louisiana State Museum for his expert curatorial advice throughout the entire process of creating this exhibition; the show is richer for his generous contributions. We are also indebted to the United States Golf Association and The Royal and Ancient Golf Club of St Andrews. As stewards of the game we love, the USGA and the Club have helped preserve the legacy of the game for future generations to enjoy.

JULIA A. FORBES
Managing Curator, The Art of Golf
Shannon Landing Amos Head of Museum Interpretation
High Museum of Art
Atlanta, Georgia

CATHERINE M. LEWIS, PH.D.
Consulting Curator, The Art of Golf
Executive Director, Museums, Archives and Rare Books, and Professor of History
Kennesaw State University
Kennesaw, Georgia

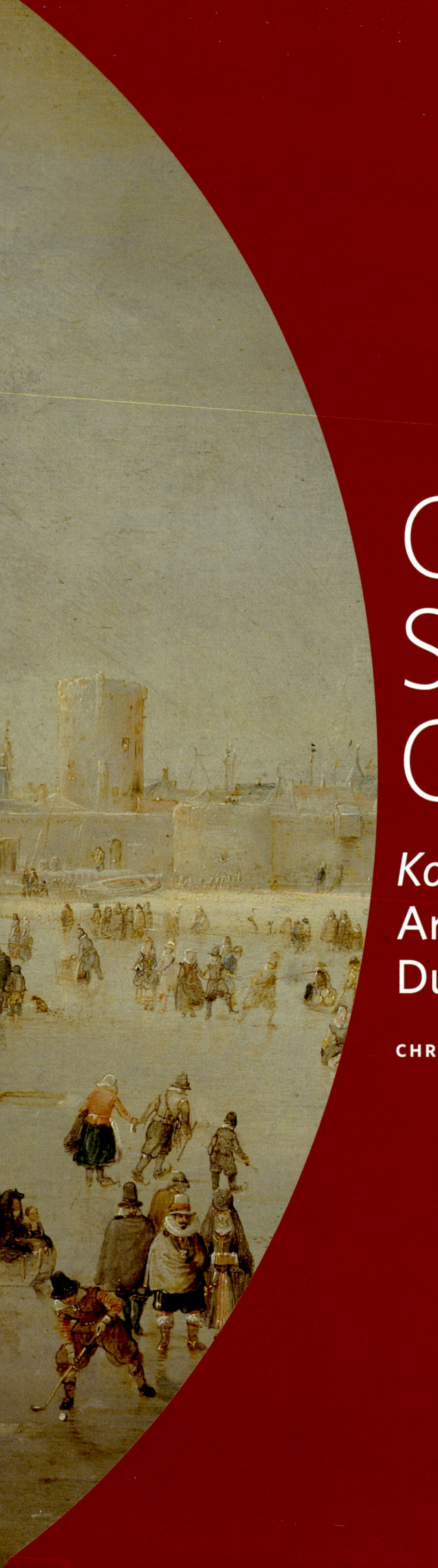

On Slippery Ground

Kolf in the
Art of the
Dutch Golden Age

CHRISTIAN TICO SEIFERT, PH.D.

JOANNES SIX VAN CHANDELIER

On his "Grand Tour" of Northern Europe from 1667 to 1669, Cosimo III de' Medici, Grand Duke of Tuscany, visited the Netherlands twice. The grand duke's official journals devote only one line to his visit to the workshop of the great artist Rembrandt; it seems Cosimo was more fascinated by the joy the Dutch took in their leisure activities on the ice, or *ijsvermaak*—literally, "pleasure on the ice." Cosimo spent New Year's Day 1668 walking on the ice in Amsterdam, marveling at "three miles [of ice] covered with numerous people of all ranks, men and women, old and young alike, with many sledges, some drawn by horses and some pushed by hand."[1] It is obvious that this made an extraordinary impression on the grand duke, who was of course used to a Mediterranean climate. While the journals do not specifically mention *kolf*, a game often cited as one of modern-day golf's antecedents, it seems reasonable to speculate that it was among the activities observed by the grand duke. Skating, sledding, and games with balls and clubs (such as *kolf*) as well as eating, drinking, and merely conversing on the ice were extremely popular with the Dutch throughout the seventeenth century and still are to this day.

Paintings from the Dutch Golden Age in the seventeenth century offer a lively visual account of the joys and risks encountered on the ice's slippery surface. The genre of the winter landscape emerged in Flemish art in the mid-sixteenth century in the circle of Pieter Bruegel the Elder (fig. 1). By the end of the sixteenth century the Netherlands

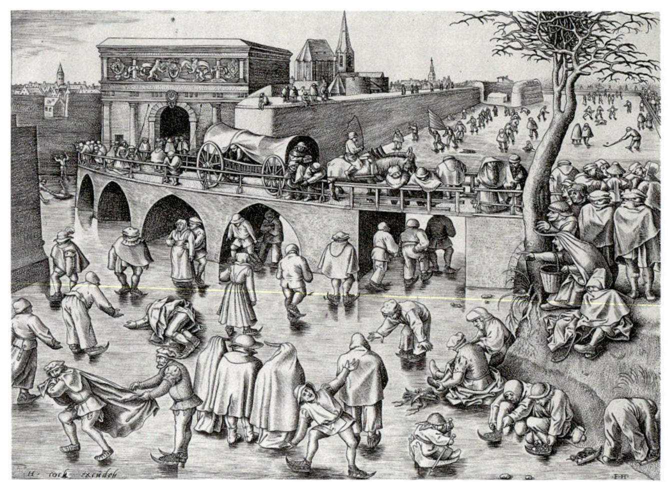

FIG. 1 Frans Huys (Flemish, 1522–1562) after Pieter Bruegel the Elder (Flemish, ca. 1525–1569), *Skating before the Saint George's Gate in Antwerp*, ca. 1559–1560, engraving, 9⅛ × 11¾ inches, The Metropolitan Museum of Art, New York.

had separated into mostly Catholic Flanders (or Southern Netherlands), ruled by the Spanish Habsburgs, and the predominantly Protestant northern provinces, including Holland, which formed the Dutch Republic. It was in Holland that Hendrick Avercamp became the unrivaled master of such winter scenes. Avercamp, who was known as "the Mute" (*de stomme*) due to his inability to speak—he was possibly even deaf-mute—spent most of his life in Kampen, a tranquil walled town on the shore of the Zuider Zee, northeast of Amsterdam. His atmospheric *Winter Landscape* (plate 1) is an especially unusual example of his artistic output in that it is painted on copper, a surface rarely used by the artist. The walled town depicted in the background was previously thought to be Kampen but is, in fact, more likely an imagined site. In the foreground four men are shown playing *kolf*: each individual equipped with a club, two teams of two players each try to hit the target—presumably the two thin tree trunks enclosed in the ice—with their ball. To discourage instances of cheating, a referee was sometimes chosen to mark the scores for

1 HENDRICK AVERCAMP (DUTCH, 1585–1634)

Winter Landscape, ca. 1610–1620
Oil on copper, 11¼ × 16¾ inches
National Galleries of Scotland, Edinburgh, NG 647

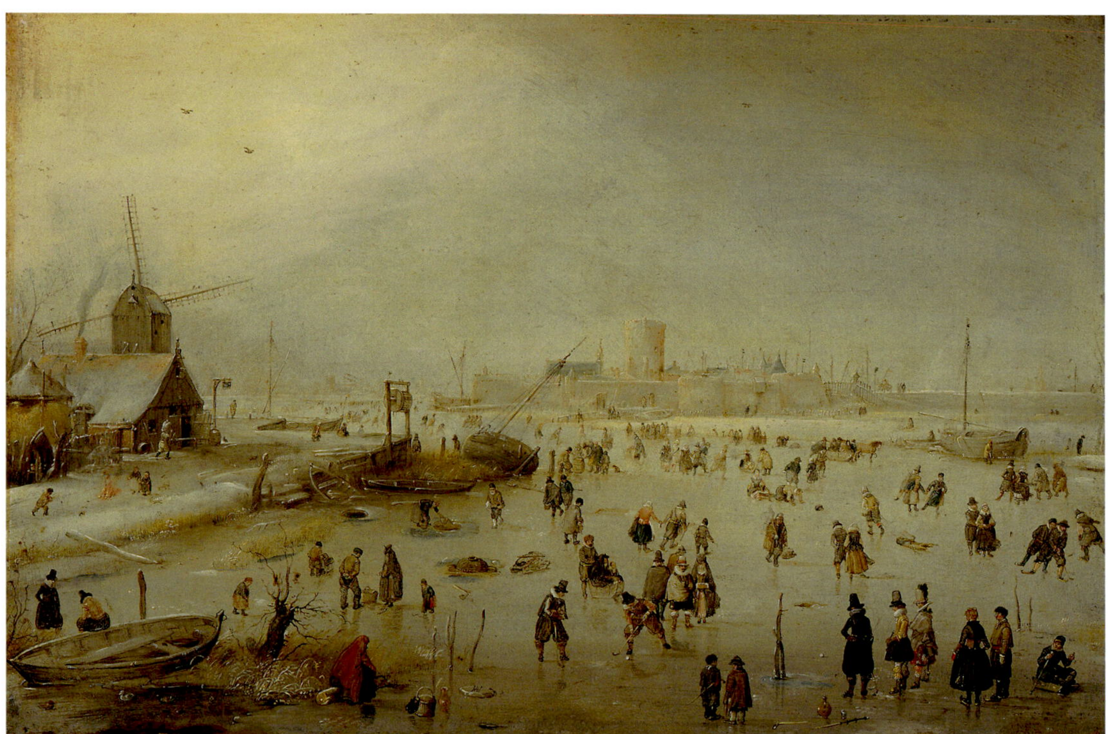

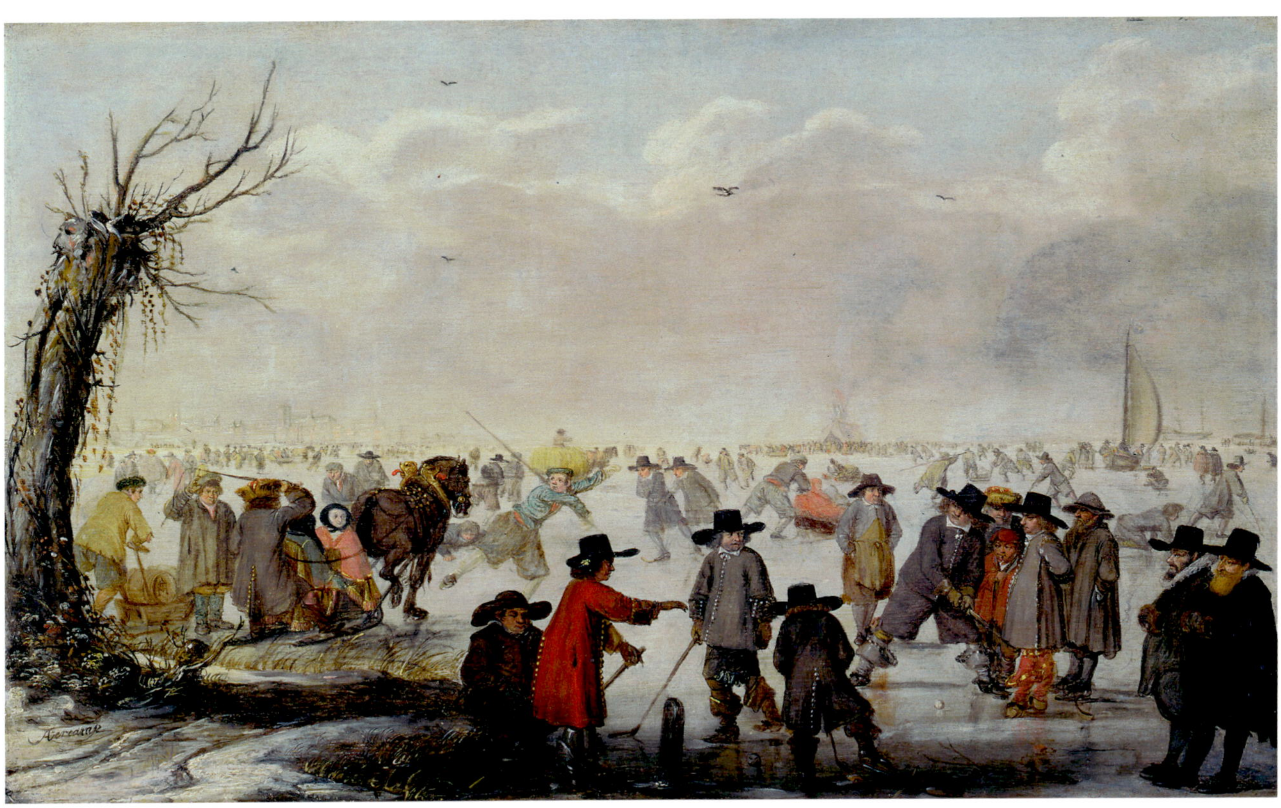

all players. The game is watched by several bystanders, among them two children, one of whom is also holding a club. This scene is similar to the one depicted in a painting in the collection of the High Museum of Art by the artist's nephew Barent Avercamp (plate 2), who is said to have trained with his uncle and whose works are sometimes confused with Hendrick's. The viewpoint of Barent's paintings, however, is usually lower than that of the elder Avercamp's works, here giving prominence to the foreground figures, who appear to be holding equipment similar to that shown in Hendrick's painting. At the far right, an ice sailing boat is depicted.

Another Dutch master of the winter landscape was Aert van der Neer, who came from Gorinchem near Dordrecht but settled as a painter in Amsterdam in 1632. By the late 1650s he was also running an inn, though it did not save him from bankruptcy—he died in poverty in 1677. Best known for exquisite moonlit landscapes, his painting *Skaters and Kolf Players on a Frozen Waterway* (plate 3) shows a group of skaters and *kolfers* on a vast icy channel under an expansive sky, which belies the painting's small size. The popularity of *ijsvermaak* is indicated by its frequent depiction in works of art. Such pictures were in high demand and produced in considerable numbers and at different levels of quality and price to suit the broad market for them. While one could argue that these winter scenes are depictions of everyday life and as such should be classified as a branch of genre painting, it was usually landscape painters who excelled in the field. As an alternative to paintings and drawings, prints met the great demand for less costly depictions of winter activities. It is worth noting that the period between 1550 and 1650, when *ijsvermaak* was especially popular and widespread, coincided with an era of particularly severe winters, a climactic

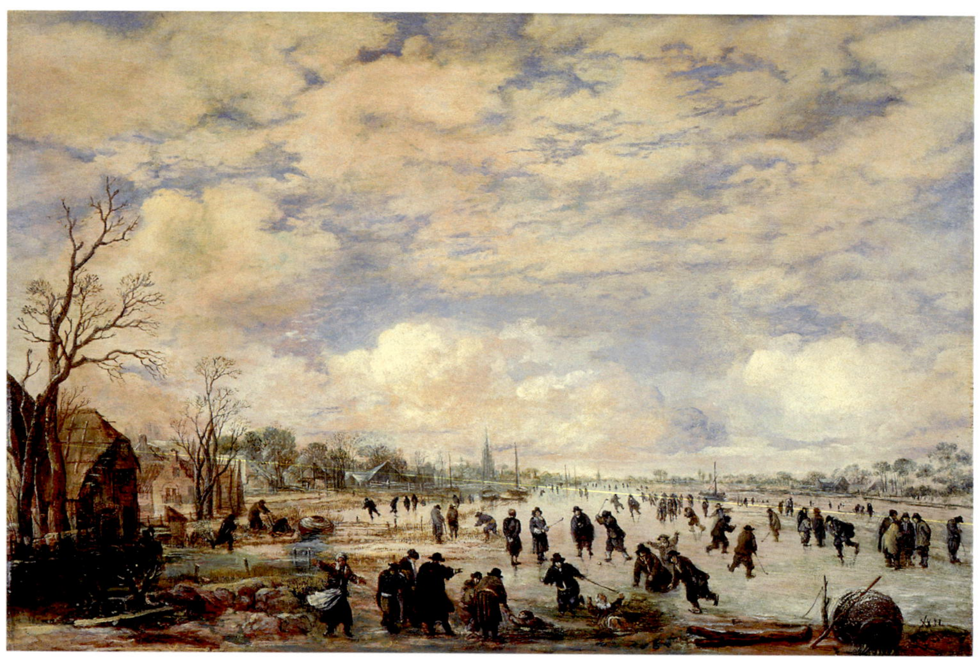

phenomenon that has been called the "Little Ice Age." It is tempting to see a relationship between the freezing winters, the subsequent fondness for leisure activities on the ice, and the emergence and popularity of the winter landscape in painting.[2]

In comparison to modern golf, which has its roots in Scotland, Dutch *kolf* seems to have been less formal and was played exclusively by males on undesignated public grounds in varying forms and with different sets of rules. Two variants of the game are described in Joannes Six van Chandelier's jocular poem "The Amsterdammer's Winter," of 1650:

> The *kolfer* ties his ice spurs on
> or finds something rough to stand on.
> Because slippery ice, if without snow,
> laughs and mocks smooth soles.
> And after the teams have been decided,
> standing surely, strikes his aspen [a type of poplar club], with lead
> weighted, or his Scottish cleek
> of boxwood, three fingers wide, one thick
> with lead in it, the feather ball
> from the tee, invisible until its fall,
> observed by ball spotters,
> further *kolfing* toward an enclosed pole.
> Or [he] strikes for the widest [distance], strike after strike
> for silver [coins], or a boozy breath.[3]

Six's description is remarkably detailed, even mentioning a Scottish type of club called a "cleek." This suggests that similar games, or at least similar equipment, were already

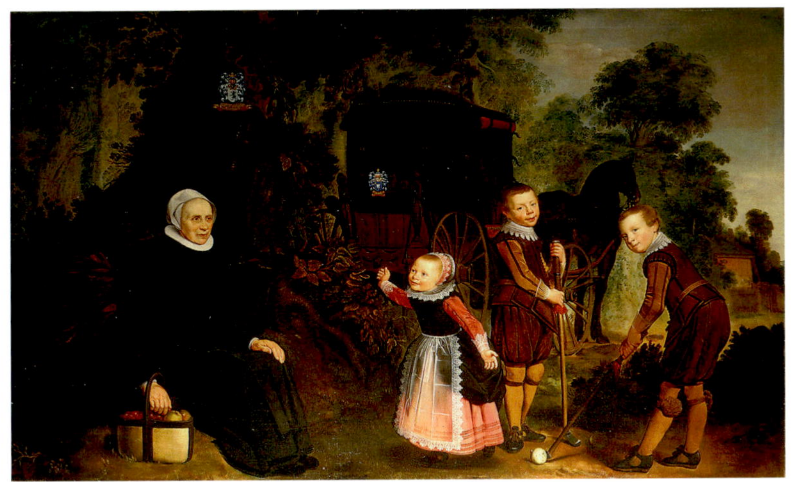

FIG. 2 Nicolaes Eliasz. Pickenoy (Dutch, 1588–1655), *Boys Playing Kolf on a Road (Portrait of Gerritgen Dircksdr Poelenburch and Her Grandchildren),* ca. 1626, Six Collection, Amsterdam.

common in Scotland during the seventeenth century. Six also refers to the players rounding off their game in a nearby inn, and indeed, pictures of *ijsvermaak* typically include a depiction of an inn or a booth on the ice where drinks could be purchased. It is also worth noting that although it was almost exclusively depicted in winter landscapes, *kolf* was played during the warmer months as well, as is evident in Nicolaes Eliasz. Pickenoy's group portrait (fig. 2). The two boys, who appear to be about seven or eight years old, seem to be ready to start a game on a warm, sunny day. In the summer, *kolf* was probably played on sandy ground rather than grass, which would have required regular maintenance.

Kolf belonged to a broad and varied family of games that involved clubs and balls, all of which can broadly be taken as antecedents of modern golf. Another popular variant was *Mail à la Chicane* (Pall Mall), which is depicted in the painting *Landscape with Men Playing "Mail à la Chicane,"* by Paul Bril (plate 4). Bril was Flemish but went to Rome around 1575. There he became a successful painter, working for popes and princes alike. Bril's painting shows Pall Mall players in a classical Italianate landscape, with the inclusion of the stall of a professional ball- and club-maker at the right. As in *kolf*, there were variations

4 **PAUL BRIL (FLEMISH, 1554–1626)**

Landscape with Men Playing "Mail à la Chicane," 1624
Oil on canvas, 26⅝ × 34¾ inches
Minneapolis Institute of Arts, Minneapolis, the William Hood Dunwoody Fund, 40.3

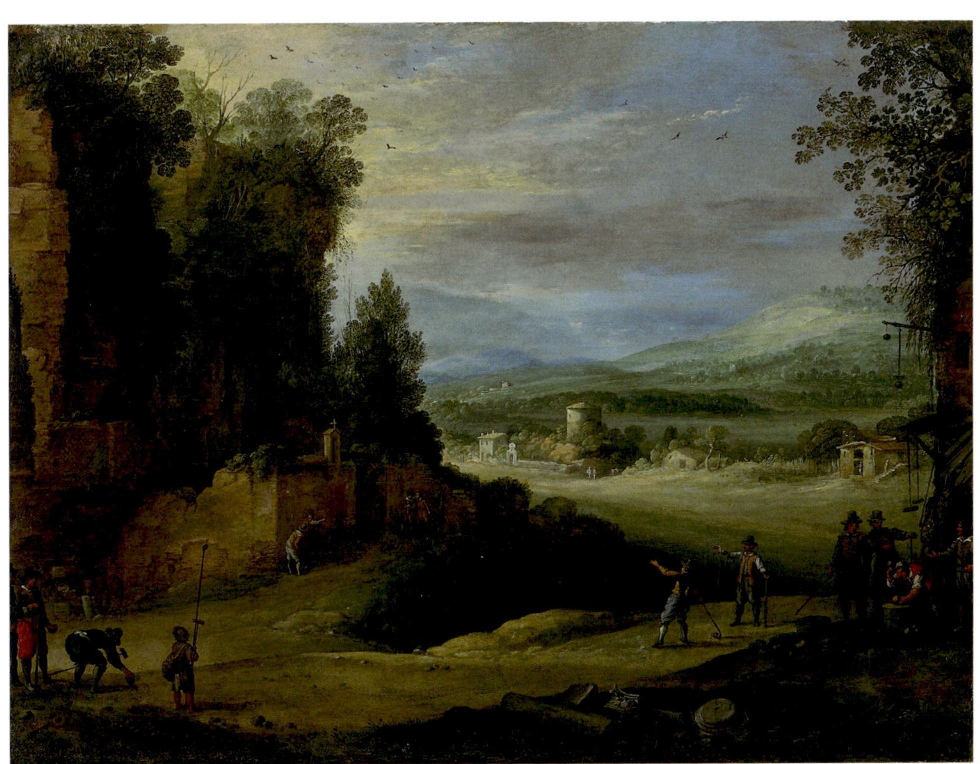

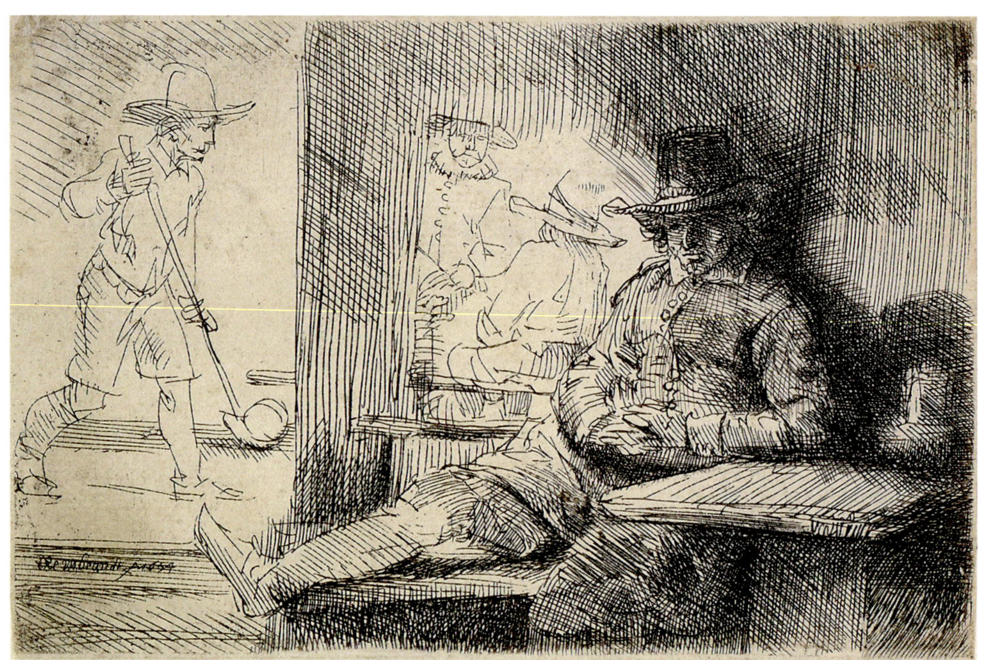

to the rules of Pall Mall, with the players either aiming at targets or driving the ball long distances. It could be played in singles or teams and—unlike the cross-country version depicted by Bril—it was played on a long, designated alleyway. Some famous street names today reveal their origins in this game, for example London's Pall Mall or The Hague's Maliebaan (fig. 3), which stretches for more than one kilometer.

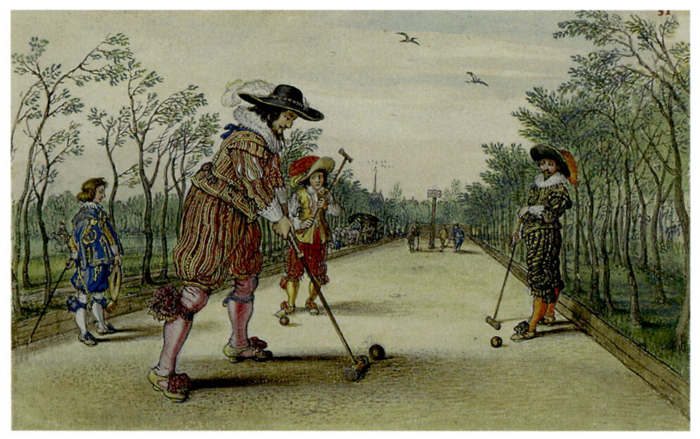

Another game related to *kolf*, "ringball" (*klossen*), is depicted in Rembrandt's famous etching of 1654 (plate 5). This print was still correctly referred to as *Het Klosbaantje* (*The Ringball Alley*) in the early eighteenth century, but later it was erroneously referred to as *The Game of Kolf*.[4] Ringball was already a popular pastime in the late Middle Ages and is still played in Holland today, though it is now called *beugelen*. The aim of this game was to hit the ball—which was considerably larger and heavier than a *kolf* ball—with a club through an iron ring on an alley, or to drive an opponent's ball into the side gutters. With a striking economy of means, Rembrandt succeeds in creating an enigmatic atmosphere. In the foreground, a man sits in contemplation at a table, most likely in a tavern. Ringball alleys were usually found at inns or taverns, as seen in a painting of 1670 by the Amsterdam painter Gerrit Lundens (fig. 4). In the background of Rembrandt's print, one man is holding a club and striking a ball, while the other two seem to be conversing with one another. The indeterminate spatial rendition, the uneven opening behind the man, the strong contrast of light and shade, and the sketchy execution of the background scene create

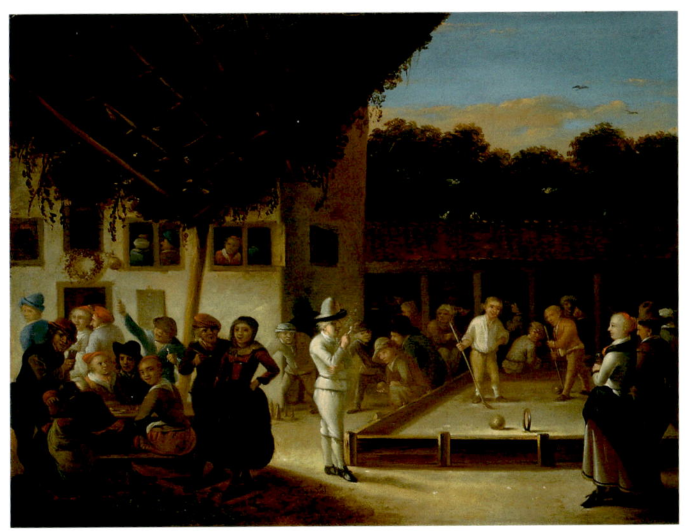

an almost dreamlike atmosphere. It is worth noting that in seventeenth-century Holland the game of *kolf* was sometimes interpreted as a metaphor for the "Game of Life," with its implications of chance and fate and the moral necessity of working toward a clear goal. Considering the contemplative mood of Rembrandt's print, it is quite possible that ringball was also interpreted in this way.[5]

The fame of Dutch winter landscapes soon expanded beyond the country's boundaries. While examining *kolf* and its relationship to modern golf, it is useful to note the historic links that existed between the Netherlands and Scotland. From the late medieval period onward there were strong ties between the two countries, based mostly on patterns of trade. Scottish wool, cloth, coal, and lead were shipped to Middelburgh and Veere in Zeeland, and later mainly to Rotterdam. Upon their return to Scotland, these ships brought with them luxury goods such as linen, silk, and spices, along with works of art. In 1647 the Scottish merchant, collector, and art dealer John Clerk of Penicuik brought a shipload of artworks to Leith, the port that served Edinburgh. Among the many objects was "1 hiver de Brugl in an eben bordeur."[6] This was probably a winter landscape by Pieter Bruegel the Younger, who followed in the footsteps of his father (see fig. 1). In 1704 the Duke of Hamilton owned a "Winterpiece with men goeing with sketts on the Ice" by an unknown, probably Dutch master.[7] We may assume that paintings like these included depictions of winter games on the ice and that at least some people in Scotland were familiar with *kolf* through these images. At the same time, an exchange of golfing equipment seems to have taken place, given that Six mentioned a "Scottish cleek" in his poem as early as 1650. The cleek was originally used as a driving iron as well as for putting. In addition to pictures, there was a steady stream of people traveling between Scotland and the Dutch Republic. The lively cultural exchange between the two predominantly Protestant countries included merchants and seamen, students, academics, and clerics—all traveling and spending time abroad. It seems highly likely that, like Grand Duke Cosimo, Scottish visitors to the Netherlands would also have marveled at the lively *ijsvermaak*, be it outdoors on cold winter days or merely in pictures. Perhaps *kolf* was the game that most piqued their curiosity.

With many thanks to Jordan Mearns for his generous and expert advice.

NOTES

1 G. J. Hoogewerff, "De twee reizen van Cosimo de' Medici Prins van Toscane door de Nederlanden (1667–1669)," *Journalen en documenten (Werken uitgegeven door de Historisch Genootschap)*, 3rd ser., 41, (Amsterdam 1919): 75. Author's translation from the Italian.

2 Pieter Roelofs et al., *Hendrick Avercamp: Master of the Ice Scene* (Amsterdam: Rijksmuseum, 2010), 23–29. See also Ariane van Suchtelen et al., *Holland Frozen in Time: The Dutch Winter Landscape in the Golden Age* (The Hague: Mauritshuis, in association with Waanders Uitgevers, 2001).

3 Joannes Six van Chandelier, *Gedichten*, ed. A. E. Jacobs (Assen: Van Gorcum, 1991), 1:113. Author's translation from the Dutch.

4 Erik Hinterding, *Rembrandt Etchings from the Frits Lugt Collection* (Bussum and Paris: Thoth, Fondation Custodia, 2008), 1:260–262, no. 106.

5 Stephanie Dickey, "'Judicious Negligence': Rembrandt Transforms an Emblematic Convention," *The Art Bulletin* 68 (1986): 253–262.

6 Julia Lloyd Williams, "The Import of Art: The Taste for Northern European Goods in Scotland in the Seventeenth Century," in J. Roding and L. H. Van Voss, eds., *The North Sea and Culture (1550–1800)* (Hilversum: Verloren Publishers, 1996), 298–322.

7 Julia Lloyd Williams, ed., *Dutch Art and Scotland: A Reflection of Taste* (Edinburgh: National Gallery of Scotland, 1992), 62.

FURTHER READING

Robin K. Bargmann, *Serendipity of Early Golf* (privately printed, 2010).

Michael Flannery and Richard Leech, *Golf Through the Ages: Six Hundred Years of Golfing Art, a Pictorial Chronicle* (Fairfield, IA: Golf Links Press, 2004).

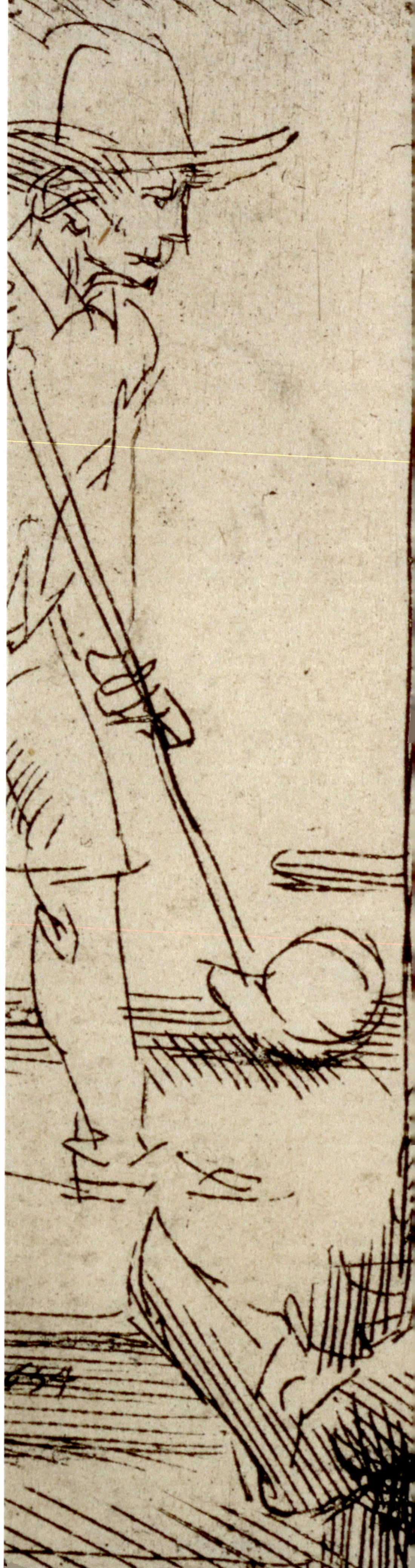

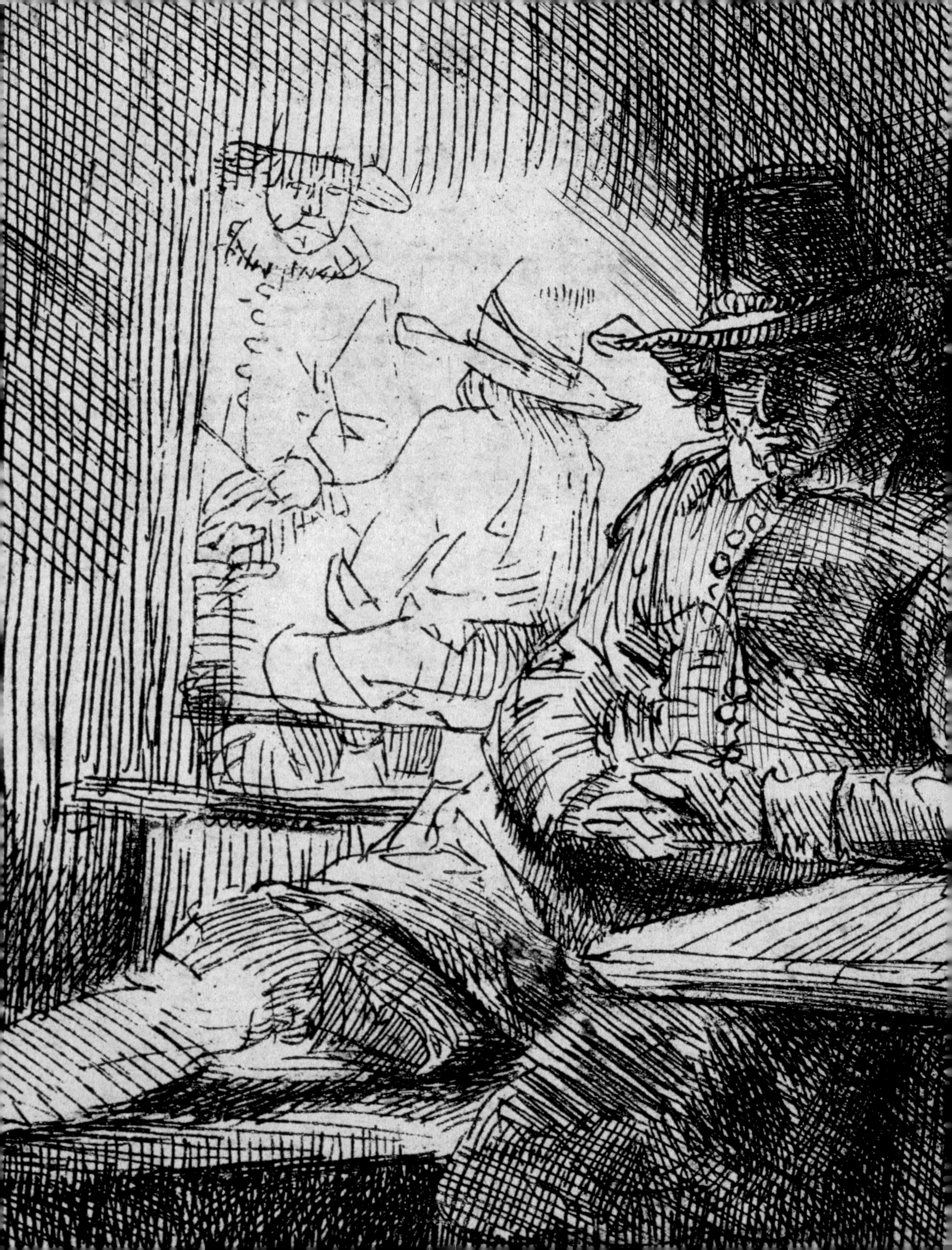

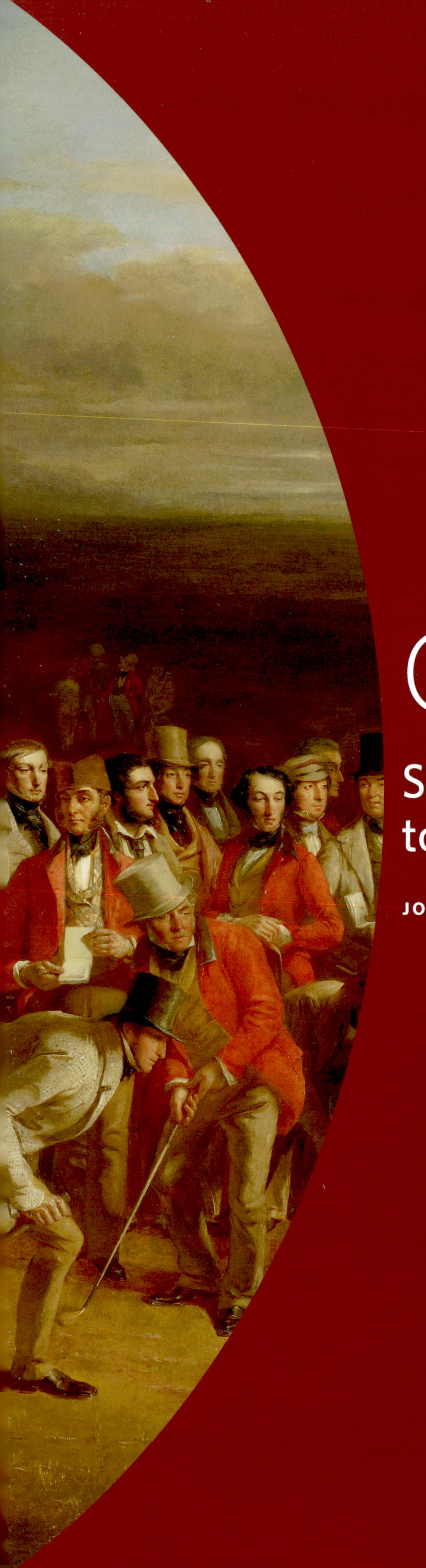

Golf

Scotland's Gift
to the World

JORDAN MEARNS

Scotland has many potent national icons: tartan kilts, bagpipes, windswept Highland castles and lochs, whisky, and golf, to name but a few. While modern Scots increasingly view these symbols as hopelessly romantic at best, or at worst as stilted and anachronistic caricatures, golf occupies a privileged and largely unquestioned place in Scottish national consciousness and sporting life. With its widespread international following, which transcends national boundaries, golf appeals to broad and geographically varied audiences, many of whom have a deep interest in the game's heritage and acknowledge that Scotland is golf's spiritual home. This essay examines key periods in the history of the game through reference to major works of golfing art created over the span of several centuries.

Early Golf in Scotland

The history of golf in Scotland begins before any images of the game were produced. The earliest accounts are literary rather than visual. These references are frustratingly slight, but they provide a vital glimpse into the game's earliest history. The first reference to golf in Scotland is found in an Act of Parliament of March 6, 1457, during the reign of King James II (1430–1460), and it is a negative one. Translated from the original Scots dialect, the act reads:

Item, it is ordained and decreed that the lords and barons both spiritual and temporal should organize archery displays four times in the year. And that football and golf should be utterly condemned and stopped. And that a pair of targets should be made up at all parish churches and shooting should be practiced each Sunday. . . . And concerning football and golf, we ordain that [those found playing these games] be punished by the local barons and, failing them, by the King's officers.[1]

During the reign of James II, Scotland faced the constant threat of invasion by its powerful southern neighbor, England. The country also was racked from within by political turmoil, including an overbearing and power-hungry aristocracy and competing political factions. Due to this fragile political situation, all boys and young men over the age of twelve were required to undertake military training in archery on Sundays after church, learning the craft of war in preparation against an invasion. Golf and other games were viewed with suspicion as a waste of time and a potentially dangerous distraction. The act quoted above was reiterated in different forms in 1471 and 1491, during the reigns of James III and James IV, respectively. The 1491 act written in the early years of the reign of James IV clearly values the defense of the realm as more important than "pointless sports":

It is statute and ordained . . . that in no part of the country should football, golf or other such pointless sports be practiced but, for the common good and for the defense of the country, archery should be practiced and targets made up in each parish under the penalty of 40 shillings to be collected by the sheriffs and bailiffs.[2]

The perceived need to reiterate Acts of Parliament banning golf attest to its popularity, but it is almost impossible to obtain a nuanced picture of the game from such brief—and negative—references. It is probable that, during this period (the last half of the fifteenth century), the game had no real fixed rules and was played with a degree of flexibility depending on the players, location, and time available.

While the political authorities tried to suppress golf, the post-Reformation Scottish church played its own part in trying to discourage the sport—especially on Sundays. From the 1580s onward, declarations were issued against golf by Kirk Sessions across Scotland. The Kirk Session consisted of elected members of the Church of Scotland and the minister (moderator), who governed the congregation with the assistance and co-operation of the ruling elders. They acted as the court of the church and were responsible for the spiritual oversight of the congregation, a duty they often performed with great severity. On February 16, 1610, the South Leith Kirk Session declared:

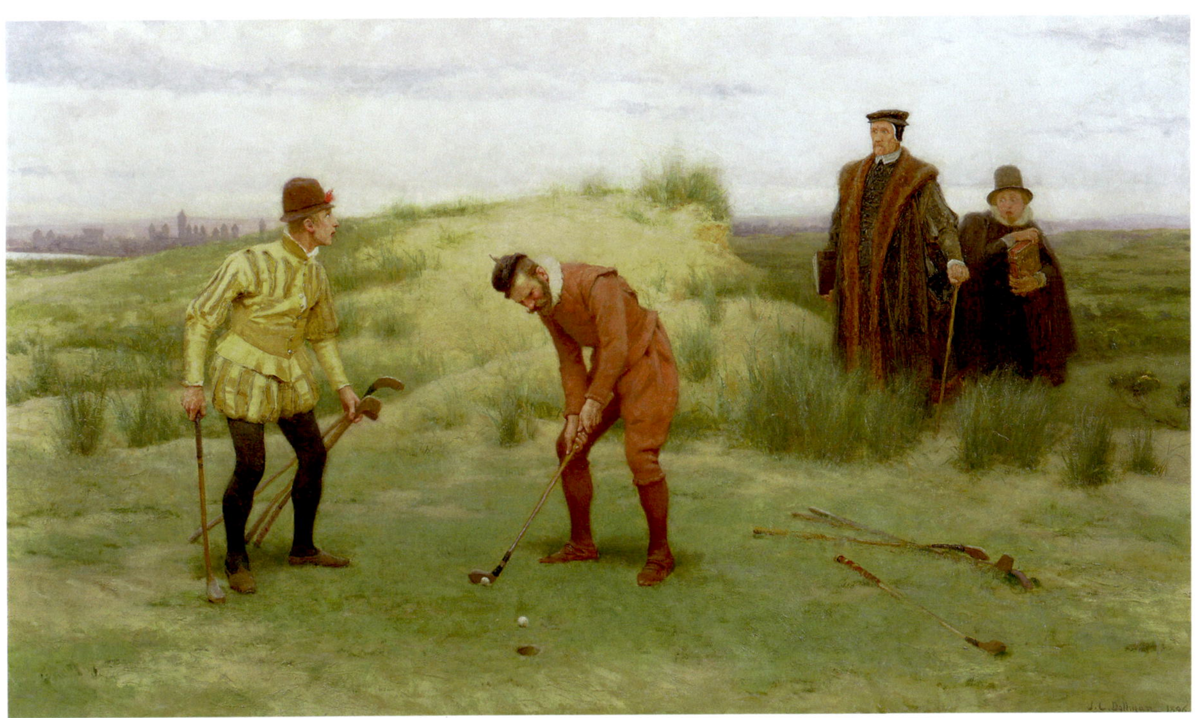

6 **JOHN CHARLES DOLLMAN (BRITISH, 1851–1934)**

During the Time of the Sermonses, 1896
Oil on canvas, 34⅛6 × 56¹¹⁄₁₆ inches
Harris Museum and Art Gallery,
Preston, United Kingdom

The said day it was concluded by the whole Session, that there shall be no public playing permitted on the Sabbath days such as playing at bowls, at the penny stone, archery, golf. . . . And if any be found playing publicly in the yard or in fields upon a Sabbath day from morning until evening they shall pay 20 shillings to the poor, and also make their public repentance before the pulpit.[3]

No images of golf exist from this period. By the late nineteenth century, however, in an age when visual reconstruction of historical events was popular, one can find images such as John Charles Dollman's fanciful painting *During the Time of the Sermonses* (plate 6), alternatively titled *The Sabbath Breakers*, which depicts an imagined scene in Scotland's distant past. In the picture a reproachful-looking Kirk elder and his assistant approach two well-dressed young men who are defying the church—skipping sermons to play a round of golf—probably with the intent of fining them.

Despite the laws and church edicts forbidding ordinary citizens from playing golf, there is evidence that royalty enjoyed the sport. James IV (1473–1513), during whose reign the 1491 act was written, flouted his own laws by playing the game. The domestic accounts kept by the Lord High Treasurer of Scotland, the functionary responsible for administering the king's wealth, suggest that James was a keen sportsman. In 1503, while the king and his peripatetic court were residing at Falkland Palace, the purchase of expensive golf clubs and balls is listed in the royal accounts. The expense of such equipment would have been out of reach of the majority of ordinary citizens, who probably made their own. The accounts also reveal the identity of one of the king's golf partners, the Earl of Bothwell. Golf as played by ordinary citizens was very different in character than that enjoyed by the social elite, not only in terms of the sophistication of the equipment used, but in the character of the game as well. The accounts imply that a wager was placed between the king and the Earl of Bothwell, which suggests that they were playing a version of the game with predetermined rules and fixed objectives.

An explanation for James IV's change in attitude toward golf can be sought in the improving political situation in the later decades of his reign. In 1502 he confirmed a peace treaty with King Henry VII, as a result of which the English king married James's daughter Margaret. Peace with England meant that military training was less essential in Scotland, making leisure and what had recently been described as "pointless sports" more acceptable.

Accounts of golf in the seventeenth century often rely on Dutch paintings of the related game of *kolf* for visual evidence. Unlike in Scotland, there was a flourishing native artistic tradition and an eager market for paintings in the Netherlands. Seventeenth-century Scotland was by no means destitute of art, but artists there tended to carry out mostly decorative and portrait commissions. There was no real Scottish equivalent to the type of descriptive genre scenes and heavily peopled landscape paintings that abound in Dutch art of this period and in which *kolf* is shown. Dutch paintings of this type may have found their way to Scotland through the extensive trading networks that existed between the two countries (as noted by Dr. Christian Tico Seifert in his essay in this volume). It is worth noting that by the mid-nineteenth century, the wealthy Scottish industrialist Frederick Bower Sharp had filled his newly built mansion, "Hill of Tarvit"—located near St Andrews

7 UNKNOWN ARTIST

View of St Andrews from the Old Course,
ca. 1740
Oil on canvas, 14 × 39⁹⁄₁₆ inches
By kind permission of The Royal and
Ancient Golf Club of St Andrews

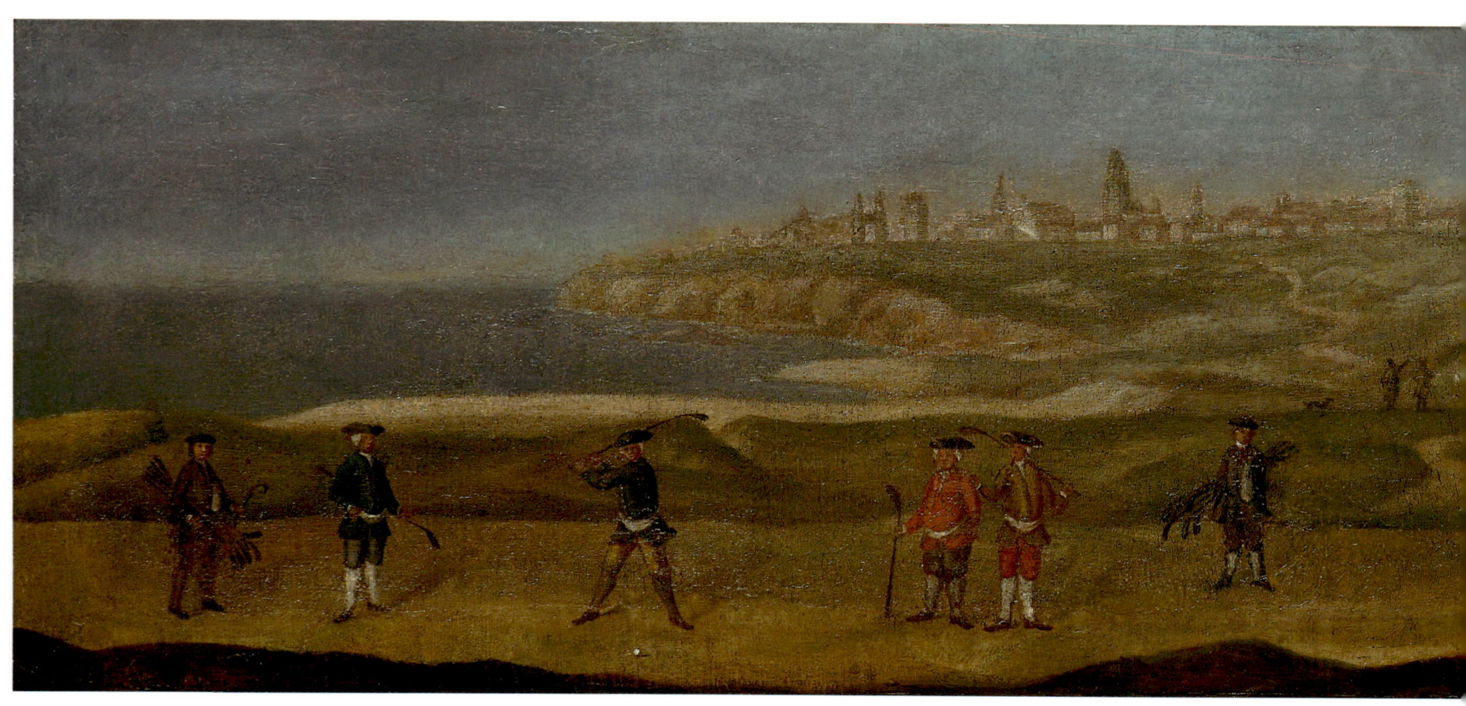

and equipped with its own nine-hole course—with Dutch Golden Age landscapes featuring *kolfers*. Perhaps he was inspired to collect such paintings precisely because of the lack of early Scottish golfing scenes.

Many historians have assumed that Scottish golf was essentially a derivative of *kolf*. Significant differences, however, distinguish the two games. In *kolf* players aimed at targets above the ground, such as poles, whereas in golf the player aimed to hit balls up to, and into, holes in the ground.

<table>
<tr><td>Eighteenth Century</td><td>

Despite more relaxed attitudes toward golf in the sixteenth and seventeenth centuries and its championing by the Scottish royal family, golf did not appear in Scottish art until the mid-eighteenth century. This was a crucial period for the development of the modern game, which saw the establishment of the first golf clubs and societies and the setting down of the written rules of the game, drawn up in 1744 by the Company of Gentlemen Golfers (now the Honourable Company of Edinburgh Golfers, based at the great course at Muirfield). The eighteenth century was a period of relative prosperity for Scotland in which the arts flourished. Despite the fact that Scotland had ceased to be an independent nation, entering into parliamentary union with England in 1707, the game remained a sport peculiar to Scots throughout this period.</td></tr>
</table>

Eighteenth Century

Despite more relaxed attitudes toward golf in the sixteenth and seventeenth centuries and its championing by the Scottish royal family, golf did not appear in Scottish art until the mid-eighteenth century. This was a crucial period for the development of the modern game, which saw the establishment of the first golf clubs and societies and the setting down of the written rules of the game, drawn up in 1744 by the Company of Gentlemen Golfers (now the Honourable Company of Edinburgh Golfers, based at the great course at Muirfield). The eighteenth century was a period of relative prosperity for Scotland in which the arts flourished. Despite the fact that Scotland had ceased to be an independent nation, entering into parliamentary union with England in 1707, the game remained a sport peculiar to Scots throughout this period.

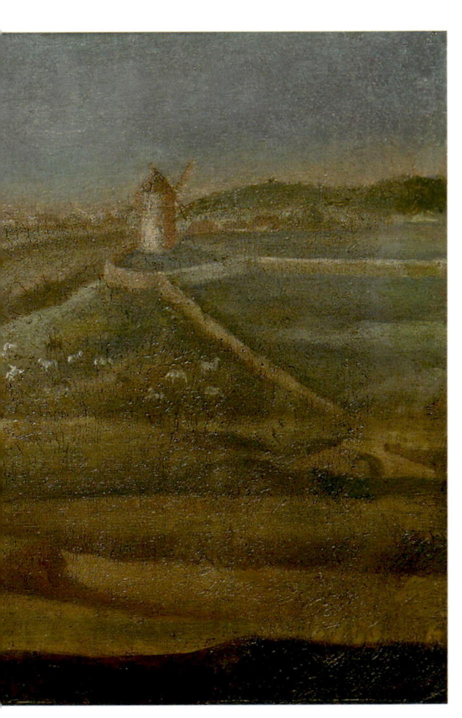

The earliest known depiction of the game in Scottish art is found in a painting belonging to The Royal and Ancient Golf Club of St Andrews. The painting (plate 7), by an unknown artist and dating from around 1740, succinctly depicts the major changes that had occurred by the mid-eighteenth century. The game as shown is in complete contrast to the bustling, hectic depictions of Dutch *kolf*, where players jostle with skaters, sledders, and all manner of simultaneous activity on the ice. Golf, on the other hand, was a sedate game, played over undulating coastal links by well-dressed, presumably wealthy gentlemen accompanied by caddies who carried bundles of clubs under their arms. The links (courses laid out along the seaside), which are so characteristic of the east coast of Scotland, were ideal for the playing of golf for a number of reasons. First, the lack of dense vegetation and undergrowth meant that the game could still be played in winter, when the grass was often frozen and stunted. The grazing of sheep on the land, as depicted in the painting, also acted as a pre-mechanical form of greenkeeping. The links were also in easy reach of the towns that line the east coast of Scotland. In the eighteenth century it was increasingly the wealthy and educated urban professional classes that shaped the game, rather than the monarchy and court.

The unusual horizontal format of the 1740 painting, combined with the fact that it is executed on a wooden panel, suggests that it may originally have been part of a decorative paneling scheme, perhaps designed to fit over a mantel or door. It depicts four golfers playing in pairs, two dressed predominantly in blue and the other two in red. While these different-colored outfits might suggest a uniform, the fact that the players are dressed this way is more likely due to the artist's desire to make the scene easily legible. Two caddies, who hold bundles of about five clubs each, accompany the players. Due to the naïveté of the painting style and the small size of the figures, an exact interpretation of the style of game play is difficult; for example, the central figure, depicted in the act of swinging, has an improbably wide-legged stance. Despite the painting's unsophisticated style and small dimensions, however, it does include an accurate view of the ancient city of St Andrews, with its romantic, ruined cathedral and university spires visible on the skyline.

William Mosman's slightly later double-portrait *Sir James Macdonald (1741–1765) and Sir Alexander Macdonald (1744–1810)* (plate 8) is a more sophisticated and highly finished painting that has become an icon of Scotland's golfing heritage. It depicts two aristocratic youngsters, the sons of Sir Alexander Macdonald of Macdonald, a great Highland chieftain with estates on the Isle of Skye. Mosman was likely born in Aberdeen around 1700, but the details of his early life are unclear. In 1732 he became a pupil of Francesco Imperiali, a famous painter in Rome, and returned to Scotland permanently in 1740. Many of Mosman's portraits feature tartan-clad sitters, and this one is no exception. The combination of three different tartans worn by the boys shows that the designation of a particular tartan to one family—a mainstay of the popular perception of Scottish national culture—had not yet been adopted.

The elder of the two boys, James, leans nonchalantly on a tree stump, holding the barrel of a rifle. His younger brother Alexander is about to drive a ball into the distant landscape. The choice of sports for each of the sitters is telling and governed by portrait conventions

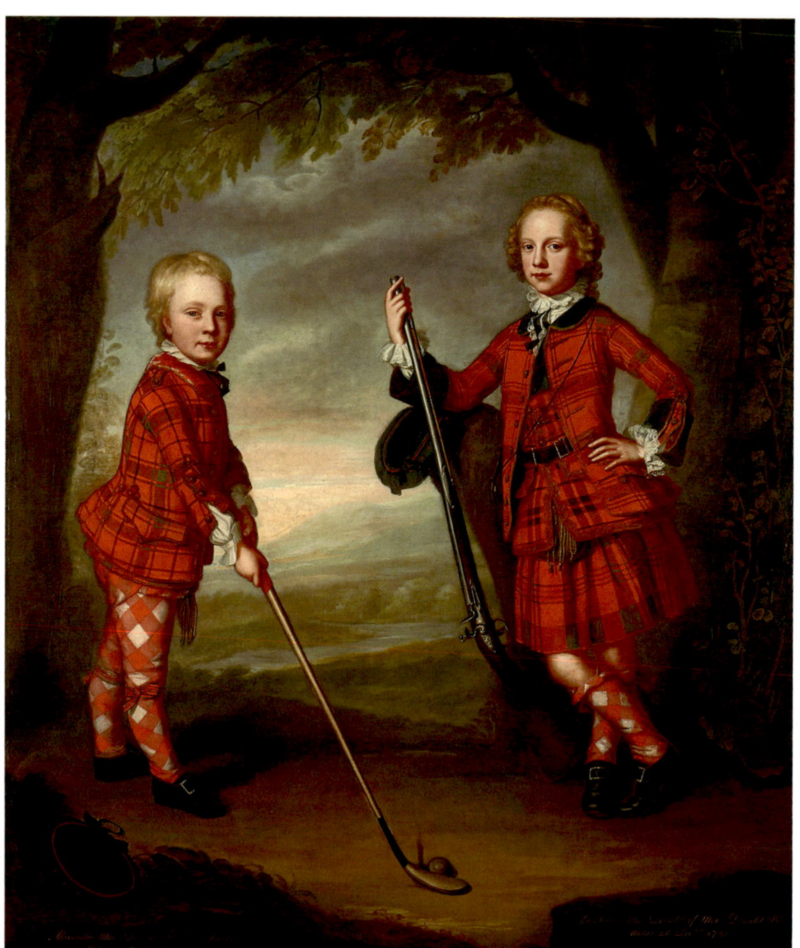

8 **WILLIAM MOSMAN (SCOTTISH, CA. 1700–1771)**

Sir James Macdonald (1741–1765) and Sir Alexander Macdonald (1744–1810), ca. 1749
Oil on canvas, 69½ × 58 inches
National Galleries of Scotland, Edinburgh, PG 2127

of the first half of the eighteenth century. James, who is about eight years of age, is closely associated with the adult and aristocratic pursuit of hunting—as befits his status as heir to his father's estate, title, and fortune. The younger son, Alexander, is depicted playing golf, which was more suitable, considering his lesser status as the junior brother. James adopts a more commanding stance than his younger brother, who is depicted "in play."

Alexander is shown holding a wooden club of long-nosed design. Clubs such as this were costly and, due to their light wooden construction, liable to wear and tear, requiring regular repairs and eventual replacement. Alexander's stance reflects the different style of play characteristic of the period. The earliest known description of golfing technique is found in the diaries of Thomas Kincaid, a young medical student who studied in Edinburgh in the mid-1680s. Kincaid's diary entry predates the first printed golf instruction manual (H. B. Farnie's *The Golfer's Manual, by a Keen Hand*, published in 1857) by 170 years. In the entry for January 20, 1687, Kincaid mused on the best technique for successful golf:

> [1] The only way of playing golf is to stand as you would do when fencing with the small sword, bending your legs a little and holding the muscles of your legs and back and arms exceeding bent or fixed or stiff and not at all slackening them in the time you are bringing down the stroke.... [2] the ball must be straight before your breast, a little toward the left foot, [3] your left foot must stand but a little before the right, or rather it must be even with it, and at a convenient distance from it, [4] you must lean mostly on the right foot, [5] but all the turning about of your body must be only...upon your legs holding them as stiff as you can.[4]

Such complex advice unwittingly anticipates the bewildering variety of "technical tips" offered in golfing manuals and videos today. Although recorded some sixty years before Mosman's portrait, the stance described in Kincaid's diary corresponds closely to that adopted by Alexander Macdonald. The boy's posture, the positioning of the ball in relation to his body, and the disposition of his feet are all in accord with Kincaid's advice. The ball Alexander is about to strike is undoubtedly a "featherie," which was manufactured by stitching three specially shaped pieces of bull- or horsehide together. This outer skin was then turned inside out so that the seams were invisible. An opening was left in one of the seams, through which wet feathers were forced until the leather was completely stuffed. As the feathers dried they expanded, and the leather shrank, forming a solid ball. While the ball was drying it could be hammered into a perfect spherical shape. Once it had completely dried out, it was coated with thick layers of white lead paint, which helped to waterproof and protect the ball and make it more visible. The raw materials used were cheap, but the extreme labor-intensiveness of the production process meant that the final product was prohibitively expensive. The high cost of featherie balls was further exacerbated by the fact that they were not very durable, became misshapen and heavy when wet, and split easily if hit with an iron-faced club.

The complex and physically demanding manufacturing process involved in crafting featherie balls is described in Thomas Mathison's poem *The Goff: An Heroi-Comical Poem in Three Cantos* (1743), which was close in date to Mosman's painting:

> The work of Bobson; who with matchless art
> Shapes the firm hide, connecting ev'ry part,
> Then in a socket sets the well-stitch'd void,
> And thro' the eyelet drives the downy tide;
> Crowds urging Crowds the forceful brogue impels,
> The feathers harden and the leather swells;
> He crams and sweats, yet crams and urges more,
> Till scarce the turgid glob contains its store.[5]

The Goff was the first book to be published solely on the subject of golf. The poem is written in a mock-heroic style, humorously mimicking the epic poetry of classical antiquity; the first line of the poem, which reads "Goff, and the man, I sing," makes a droll reference to the opening of Virgil's *Aeneid*, "a tale of arms and of a man I sing." Although the marriage of golf and high-flown poetry has resulted in dense, ponderous verse, especially to modern tastes, the poem is important for the insight it gives into the sort of person who was interested in golf in the mid-eighteenth century. The fact that the poem makes allusions to Roman poetry throughout suggests that its initial readers, presumably mostly golfers, were sufficiently educated to understand the author's witty references. This marked a shift from the ordinary, uneducated citizens the earlier Acts of Parliament had tried to ban from playing golf. Mathison's focus on the intensively physical and laborious process of ball production makes use of words whose meanings are now obscure. The "brogue" mentioned in the above excerpt was an implement strapped to the ball-maker's chest and had a blunt, protruding spike. This spike was used to force feathers into the leather skin using the full body weight of the ball-maker. Not until the introduction of "gutta percha" balls in the late 1840s would golf balls become cheaper and more durable and fly farther.

The earliest known rules of golf were drawn up by the Company of Gentlemen Golfers of Edinburgh in 1744 for the world's first open golf competition at Leith, the port of Edinburgh. On March 7, 1744, an act from Edinburgh's town council noted that "several gentlemen of honour, skillful in the ancient and healthfull excersise [*sic*] of the golf, had from time to time applied to several members of the council for a silver club to be annually played for on the links of Leith." In response to this request the council provided a silver club, which in return required that the Gentlemen Golfers should draw up "Such Articles and Conditions, as to them Seem'd most Expedient, as proper Regulations," which would govern the competition.[6]

The Gentlemen Golfers complied and drew up a detailed document outlining every aspect of the competition, which was to be open to "Noblemen or Gentlemen, or other golfers, from any part of Great Britain or Ireland." In order to be eligible to play, contenders were obliged to pay "five shillings sterling" and enter their names on a register in the eight days preceding the competition. Pairs of names drawn out of a hat determined the order of play. To ensure fair play each pair of players was to be accompanied by a "clerk" to note their scores and guard against cheating. Once the scores had been scrutinized, the player who "shall appear to have won the greatest number of holes shall be declared the winner." The silver club, which remained the property of the town council, was to be given to the winner until the next competition. He would be entitled to style himself the "Captain of the Golf," a prestigious

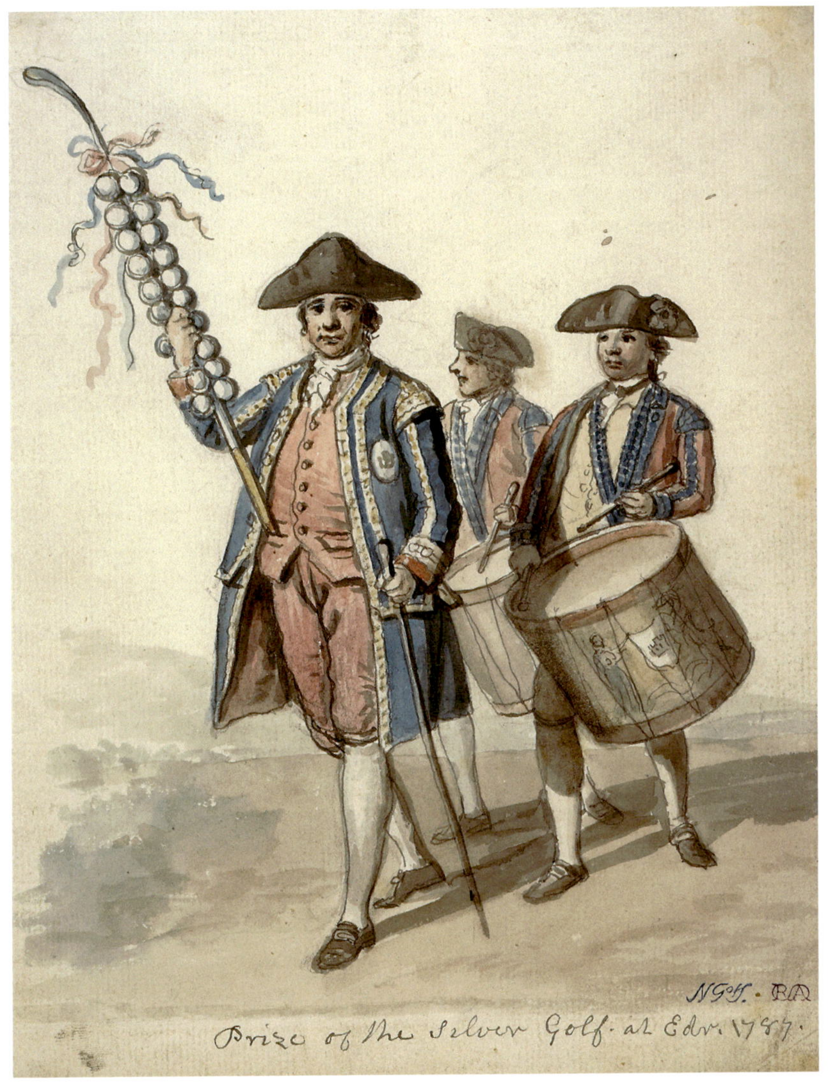

9　**DAVID ALLAN (SCOTTISH, 1744–1796)**
The Prize of the Silver Golf, ca. 1785
Black ink, pencil, and watercolor
on paper, 8½ × 6½ inches
National Galleries of Scotland,
Edinburgh, D 387

position that entailed "care and inspection of the links" and the power to act as mediator in "disputes touching the Golf, amongst golfers."[7]

These original rules were thought to have been lost, but in 1937 they were rediscovered on the last two pages of the Honourable Company's original minute book. The pages contained the thirteen articles and the signature of John Rattray, the first winner, who was Captain of the Golf in 1744–1747 and 1751. A decade later, in 1754, the golfers at St Andrews, who would become The Royal and Ancient Golf Club of St Andrews, adopted these rules almost verbatim for their own annual competition.

One of the rituals that attended the competition was that, on the day of the contest, the silver club was to be carried by the "tuck of drum" through the streets of Edinburgh to Leith Links. David Allan's drawing *The Prize of the Silver Golf* (plate 9) depicts this

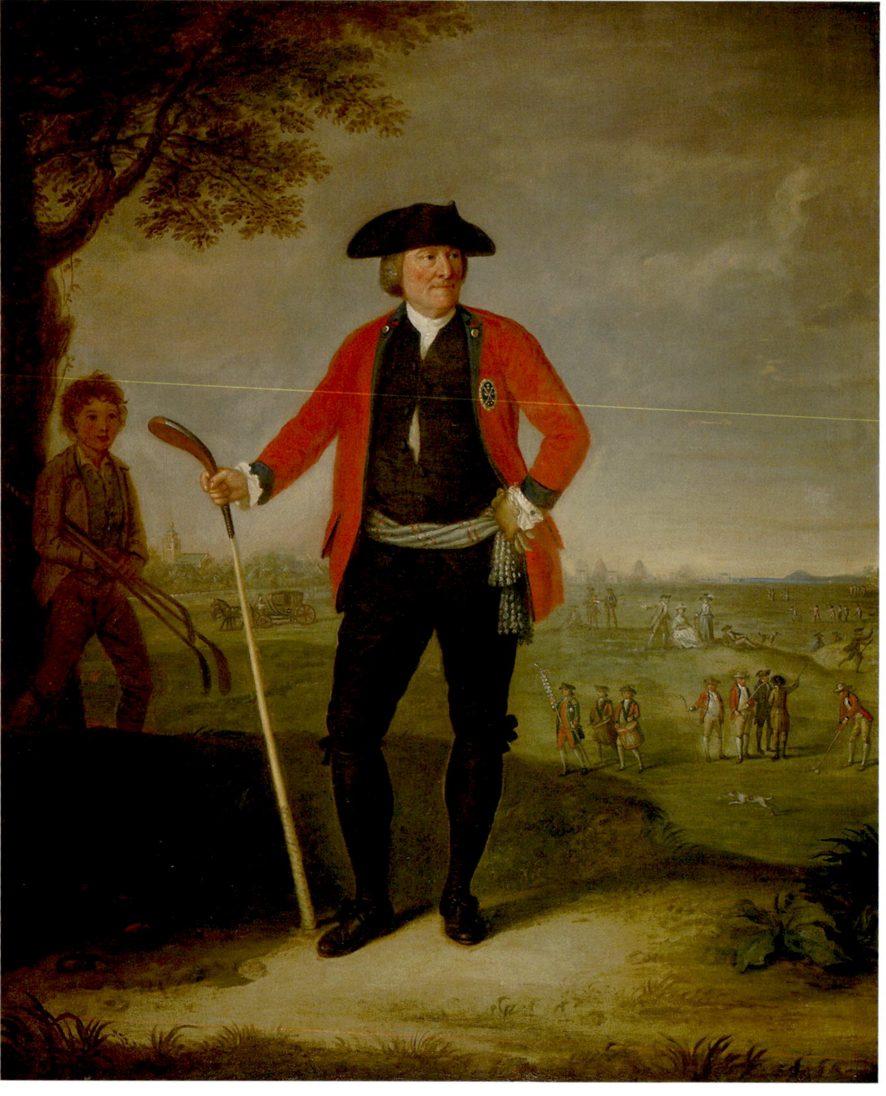

ceremony. A smartly uniformed figure, Edinburgh's Town Officer, brandishes the trophy, draped in festive red and blue ribbons, accompanied by two drummers, whose commotion alerted citizens of the imminent competition. The number of balls attached to the club signifies the long period and number of winners that had elapsed between the first contest and Allan's drawing. The drawing is one of a series that Allan made of instantly recognizable characters and incidents seen in the environs of Edinburgh.

The same figure group is repeated in the background of Allan's formal portrait of William Inglis, a notable golfer (plate 10). Inglis, like Rattray, was a surgeon, and was elected president of the Royal College of Surgeons three times. In his spare time he was an avid golfer and captain of the Honourable Company of Edinburgh Golfers from 1782 to 1784. Allan, who was a member of the same golf club, painted Inglis wearing the uniform of the Honourable Company, accompanied by a young caddie, who holds his clubs. They are shown on Leith Links, about two miles from Edinburgh. The presence of the procession of the silver club in the painting's background suggests it was a competition day.

William Inglis also sat for Sir Henry Raeburn for a picture that celebrated his golfing prowess with the silver club displayed prominently on the table at his side (plate 11). Raeburn, whose obituary claimed that he was a keen golfer, was the foremost Scottish portraitist of the late eighteenth and early nineteenth centuries. The portrait was commissioned soon after Raeburn had returned in 1787 to Edinburgh from Rome, where he, like many Scottish artists, had spent a long period of time studying the Italian Old Masters and learning from the thriving circle of expatriate artists who resided in the city. The portrait of Inglis was one of the first commissions that Raeburn received on his return to Edinburgh, and it helped establish his reputation there. He was renowned for his ability to capture his sitter's character as well as his likeness in paint, and his portrait of Inglis exudes a surer sense of the golfer's personality than Allan's rather stiff portrait. The Harveian Society of Edinburgh, of which Inglis was a founding member, probably commissioned the portrait. Founded in 1782 to "foster a kindly feeling among members of the medical profession," the society was named after William Harvey, a seventeenth-century physician who was instrumental in discovering the circulation of the blood.[8] The portrait therefore

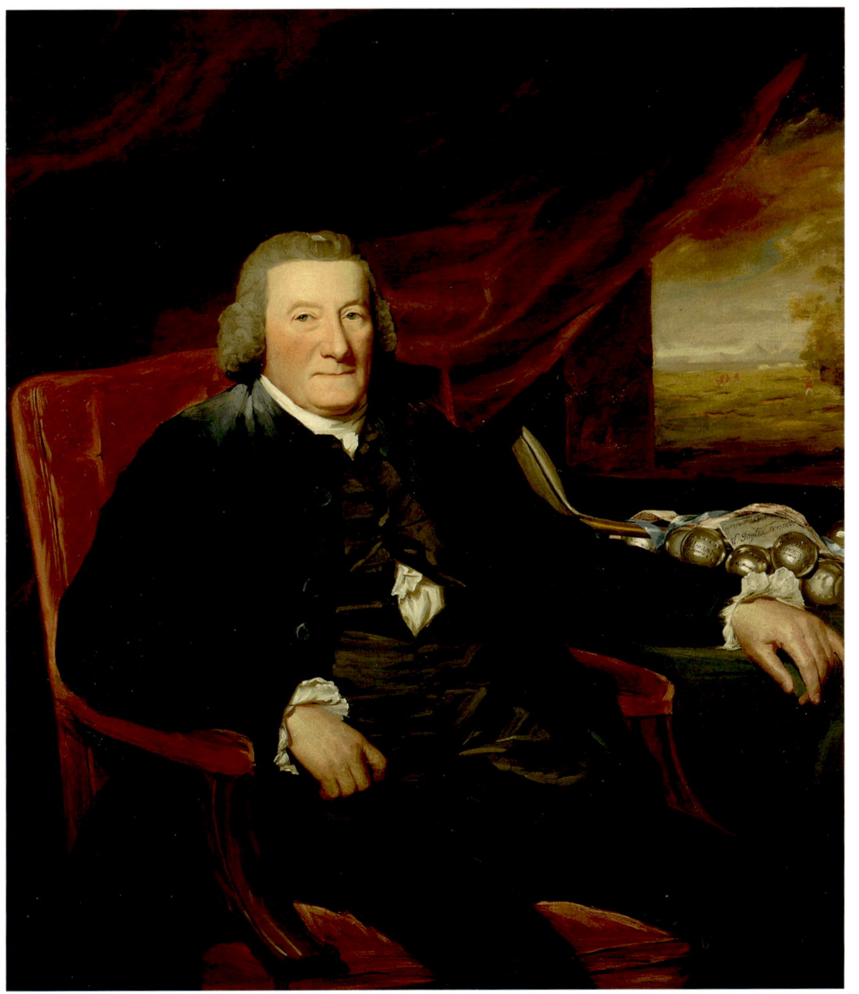

William Inglis (ca. 1712–1792), Surgeon and Captain of the Honourable Company of Edinburgh Golfers, ca. 1790
Oil on canvas, 55¼ × 47¾ inches
On loan to Scottish National Portrait Gallery, Edinburgh, The Honourable Company of Edinburgh Golfers, PGL 343

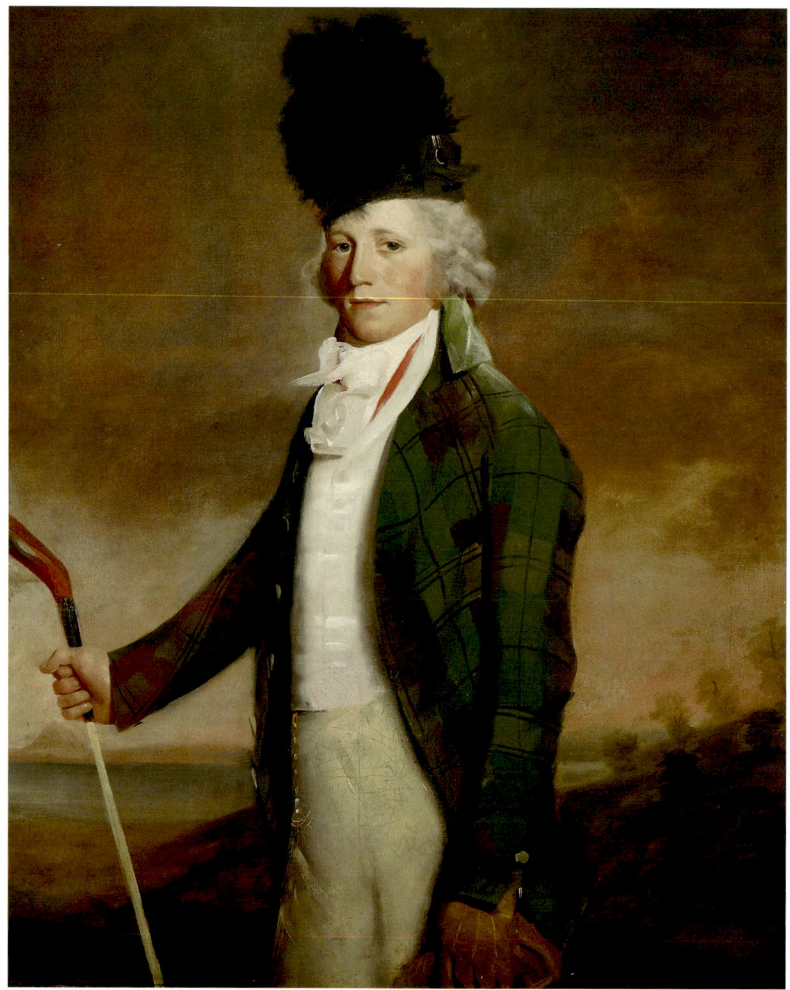

commemorates Inglis's contributions to both medical science and sport and underlines the culture of "clubbability" that thrived among professional men in Scotland at the time.

Raeburn also made a portrait of John Campbell of Sadell (1794–1859) (plate 12), who is featured prominently in Charles Lees's *The Golfers*. Legend holds that no man hit a golf ball as far as Campbell, as referenced in George Fullerton Carnegie's famous poem *First Hole at St Andrews on a Crowded Day*: "he'll engage to drive as long a ball as any man alive!"

Sir Francis Grant and Charles Lees

The central section of the *Art of Golf* exhibition is dominated by two commanding nineteenth-century scenes of golf matches: Sir Francis Grant's *Golf at North Berwick* and Charles Lees's *The Golfers*. Both depict crucial moments in foursome matches. Unlike earlier eighteenth-century portraits, in which the subjects were rather statically posed, the golfers in these pictures are portrayed "in action."

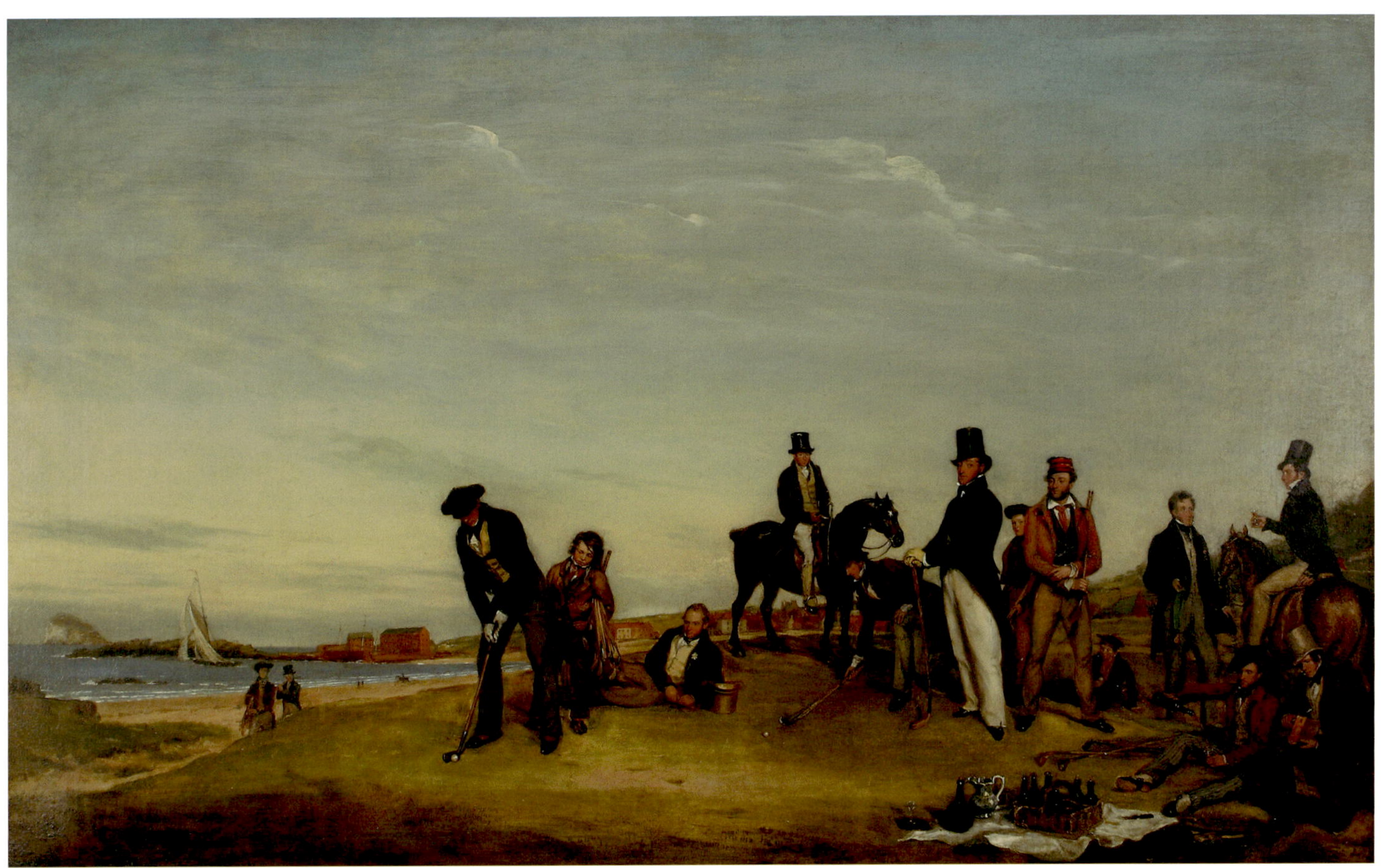

Golf at North Berwick, ca. 1832–1833
Oil on canvas, 30¾ × 44¾ inches
Private collection, New York

Sir Francis Grant became one of Victorian Britain's most fashionable society portraitists and was also noted for his equestrian and sporting scenes, in which he captured the elegant, equestrian world of hunting and race meets. He was the younger son of a prosperous land-owning family from Perthshire, and his elite social background, coupled with a suave manner, eased his ascent in the nineteenth-century art world. *Golf at North Berwick* (plate 13) is one of his earliest major works and was exhibited at the recently founded Royal Scottish Academy in Edinburgh in the spring of 1833. It features the first match played at North Berwick Golf Club, founded in 1832, of which Grant was himself a member.

The scene is set on what is today the first green at North Berwick, known as the "High Green." The landscape in the background has remained largely unaltered. A group of ten well-dressed gentlemen is shown, of whom only four are players. On the left of the green, in the act of putting, is Robert Oliphant of Rossie. The figure in the center of the canvas, incongruously dressed to modern eyes in a top hat and leaning majestically on a club, is Sir David Baird, the club's first captain. Ranald MacDonald of Clanranald stands behind Baird with club and ball in hand, having presumably just finished the hole. The assemblage of onlookers who focus on the shot being made is drawn from the ranks of the Scottish gentry closely related both to the club and to Scottish golf in general. A figure of particular interest is George Fullerton Carnegie, who sits with bottle in hand on the green on the right side of the painting. Carnegie was the author of *Golfiana or Niceties connected with the Game of Golf* (1833), a collection of poems dedicated to "the members of all golfing clubs,

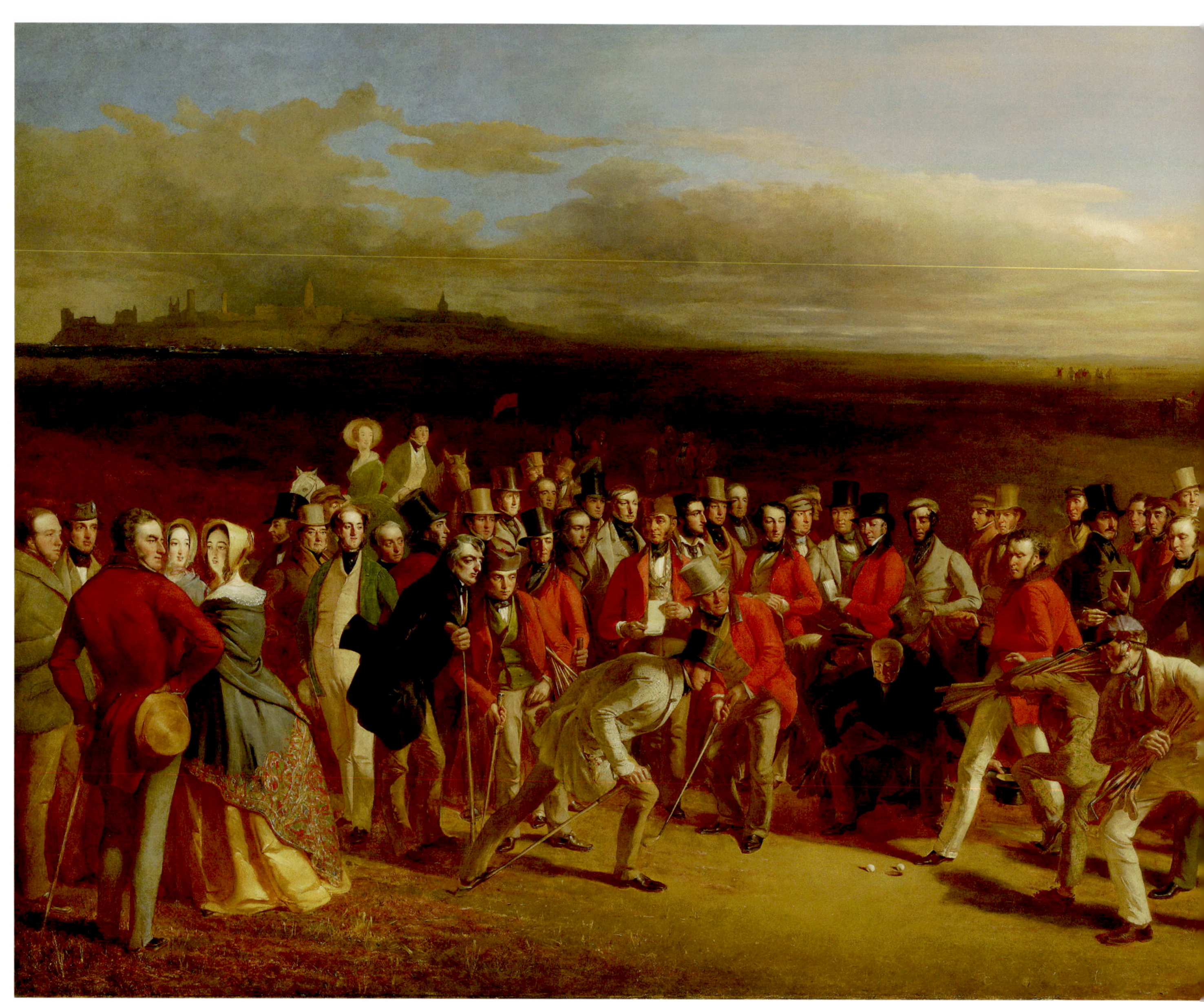

and to those of St Andrews & North Berwick in particular." Carnegie's poems paint a vivid picture of nineteenth-century golf and include witty descriptions of twenty-five eminent golfers of the day, providing glimpses into their reputations as golfers and personalities. In one of these poems, "The Golfiad," Carnegie charts the positive effects that the new golf club had on the once sleepy and unsophisticated provincial town of North Berwick, which is situated on the coast roughly twenty miles south of Edinburgh:

> Balls, clubs, and men I sing, who first, methinks
> Made sport and bustle on North Berwick Links,
> Brought coin and fashion, betting and renown,

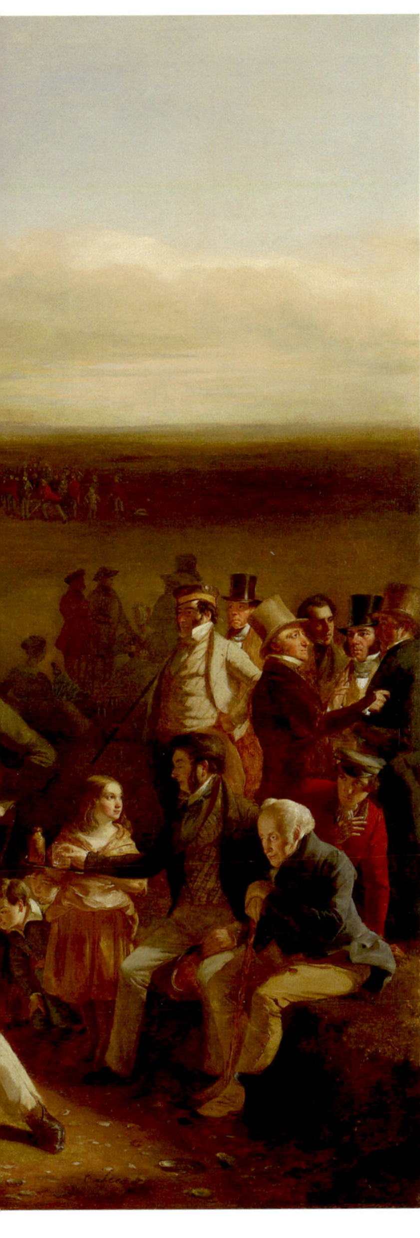

About ten years after Grant painted his North Berwick scene, Charles Lees embarked on the creation of what is considered by many to be the greatest of all golfing pictures, *The Golfers* (plate 14). Lees was born in 1800 in Cupar in Fife, a small town close to St Andrews, and in his youth studied painting in Edinburgh under Sir Henry Raeburn. Lees also spent time in Rome, then the most prestigious training ground for aspiring artists. Upon his return to Scotland he established himself as a painter in Edinburgh and exhibited regularly at the Royal Scottish Academy. He displayed many types of pictures but achieved a particular reputation for sporting subjects. Lees was particularly interested in typically Scottish sports; his sporting scenes include *The Grand Curling Match at Linlithgow* (1861), *Shinty—Scene on the Ice at Duddingston* (1861), and *Hockey on the Ice at St Marga-ret's Loch* (1864). Among his other golfing pictures are *At Bruntsfield Links* (1855), *Summer Evening on Musselburgh Links* (1860), and *Golfers Going Out on Leven Links* (1864).

The Golfers is a large and commanding painting with a densely woven and interlocking composition of fifty-four figures clustered tightly around the central scene: a two-ball foursome match in which two Scottish baronets, Sir David Baird and Sir Ralph Anstruther, take on Major Hugh Lyon Playfair and John Campbell of Glensaddell. Although there are no surviving records of this match, there is no reason to suppose that it did not take place. Interestingly, of the fifty-four portraits in the picture, twenty were described in the poems of Carnegie mentioned above. With their vivid descriptions of character and golfing prow-ess, the poems may even have inspired Lees's approach to the subject.

A full description of the painting's narrative was printed in the press to advertise the release of a popular print (plate 15) after the painting that was issued in 1854:

> The ball nearest the hole has been played by Sir David Baird, with the cleek, out of the long grass and heather on the left of the picture. The stroke, always a difficult one in such cir-cumstances, has been dextrously and well played. The ball has run over the top of the hole and lain close at the side. The other ball is supposed to be in the act of running straight for the hole, the putt having just been made by Major Playfair. The gaining of this hole being an object of interest at this crisis of the match, it is the point of time chosen by the artist as the subject of the picture.[10]

Among the figures included in Lees's canvas are John Grant of Kilgraston, Sir Francis Grant's elder brother and heir to his father's estates, and the aforementioned Sir David

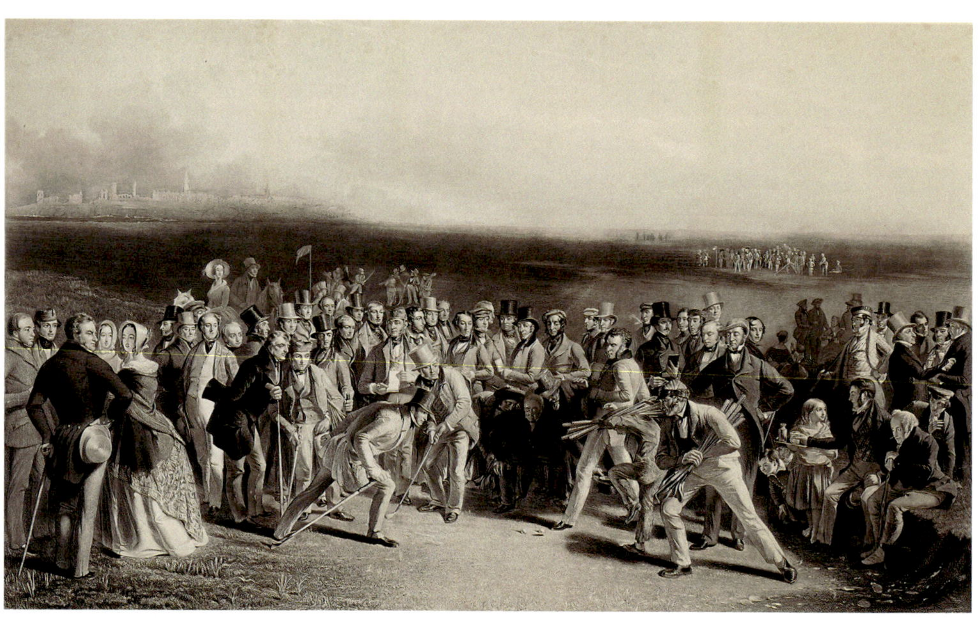

Baird, the first captain of the North Berwick Golf Club, who is the top-hatted figure in Grant's *Golf at North Berwick* (see plate 13). Baird was captain of The Royal and Ancient Golf Club of St Andrews in 1843 and won the royal medal twice, in 1841 and 1850.

The enormous complexity of the painting meant that Lees had to plan it meticulously; there are, therefore, many preparatory sketches. Lees made individual portrait studies of all the main figures. He also seems to have been fascinated with the then fashionable pseudo-science of physiognomy—the belief that the character, personality, and emotions of a person could be easily read from his face. Lees depicts a wide range of emotions— deep concentration, excitement, tension, absorption, and arrogance all feature on the spectators' faces. Full-length studies of the golfer Sandy Pirrie (plate 16), who stands just to the right of the center of the painting with a bundle of clubs under his arm, and the golf-ball-maker Allan Robertson (plate 17)—both of whom occupy conspicuous positions in the foreground of the painting—also survive. Aside from single-figure studies, Lees executed two fuller compositional studies. Both of the studies in the exhibition contain far fewer figures than the finished painting.

The most innovative compositional aid that Lees employed in the planning of the painting was photography. The earliest known photograph of golf (plate 18), showing a match in progress, was taken in St Andrews around 1845 by the Scottish partnership of Robert Adamson and David Octavius Hill. Adamson was a pioneering professional photographer who set up business in Edinburgh in March 1843. His brother John, who was involved in the early experiments with photography in St Andrews, taught him the calotype process. Shortly after opening his studio on Calton Hill in Edinburgh, Adamson met the painter David Octavius Hill.

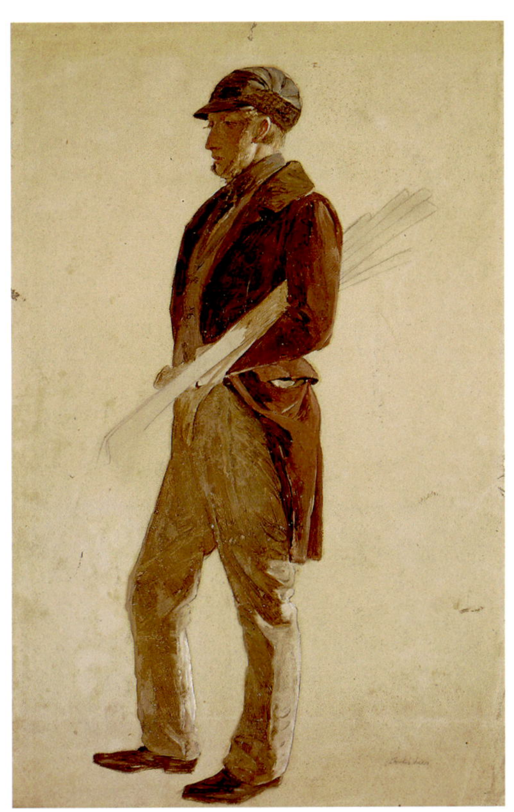
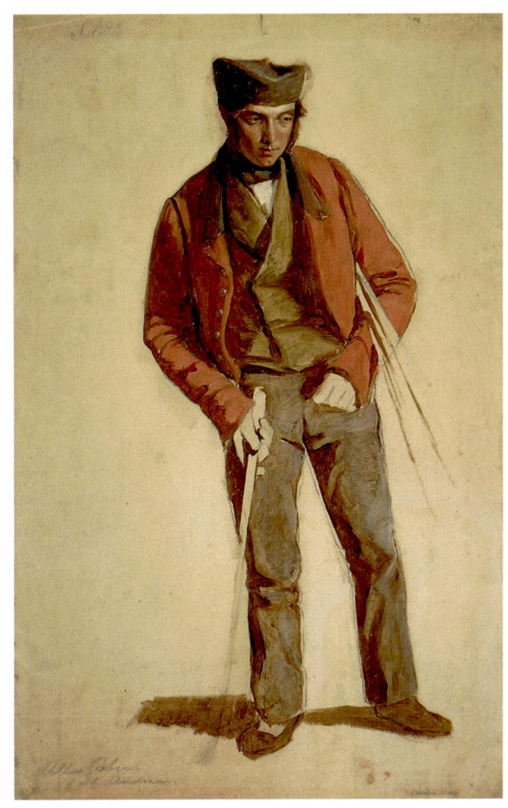
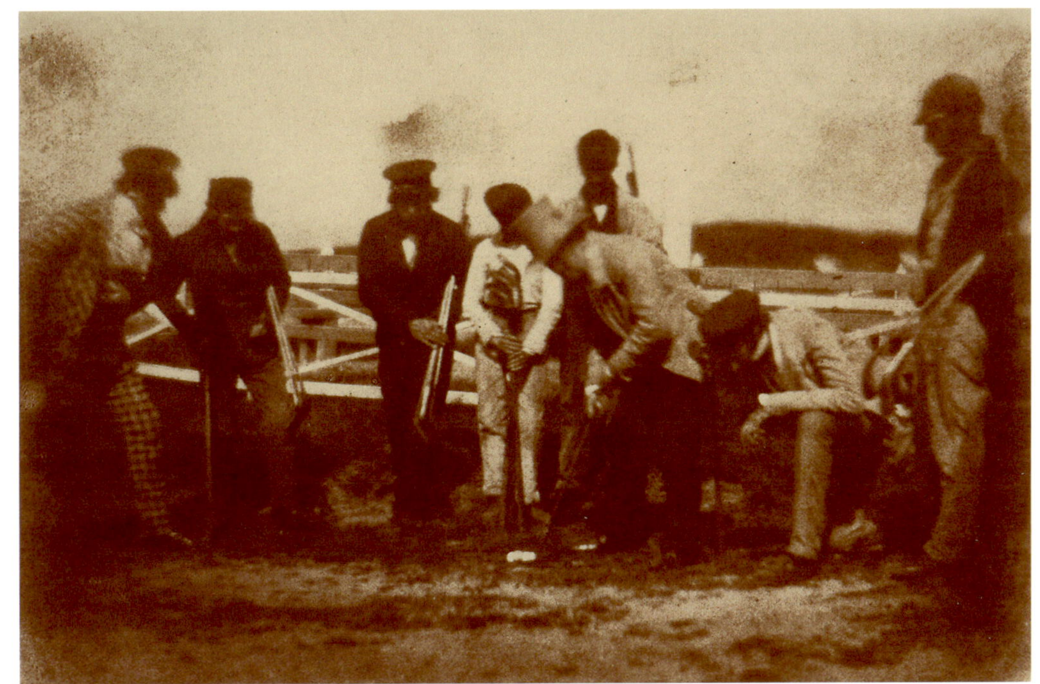

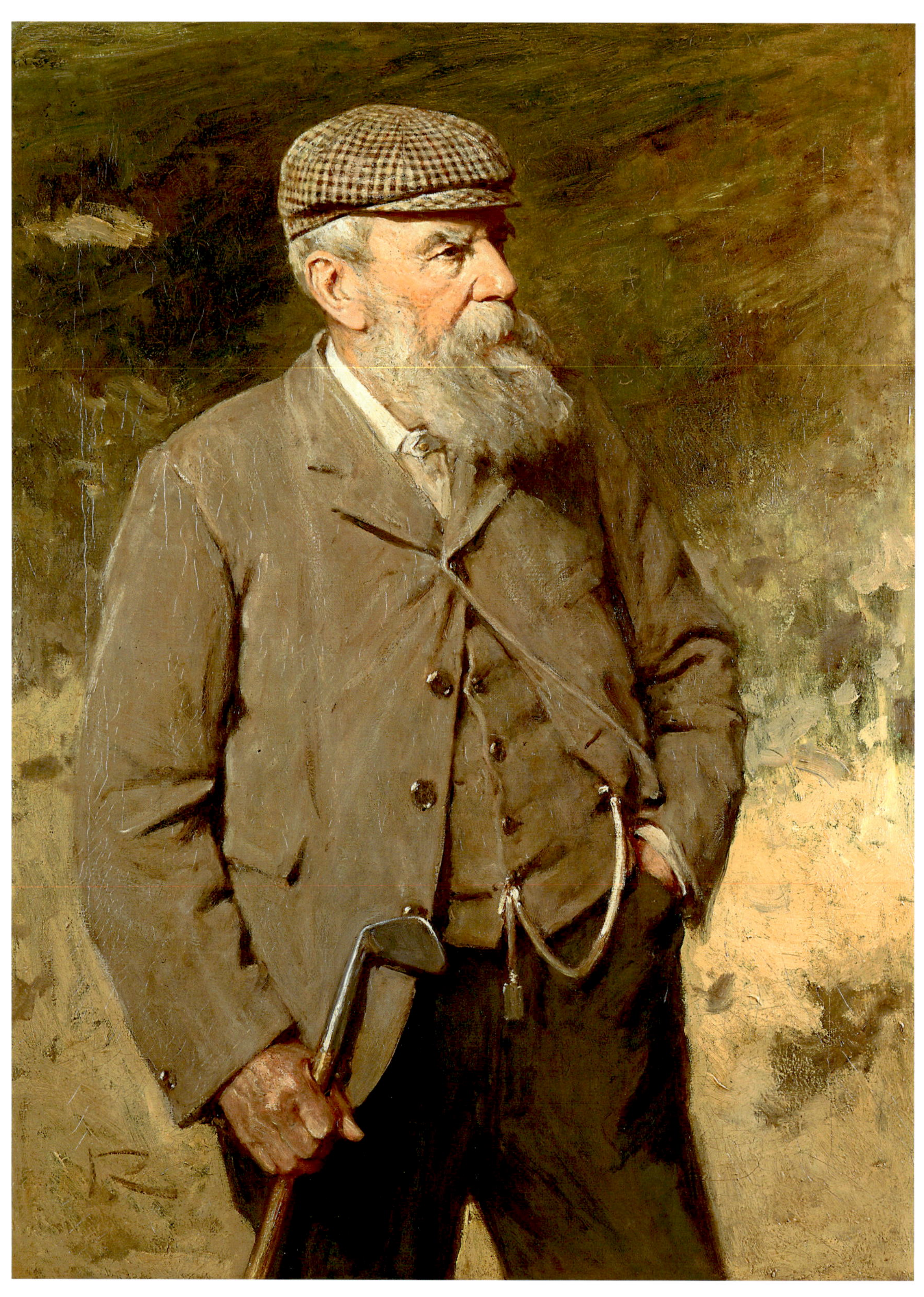

19 SIR GEORGE REID (SCOTTISH, 1841–1913)

Tom Morris, Sr., 1903
Oil on canvas, 60⅜ × 44⅜ inches
By kind permission of The Royal and
Ancient Golf Club of St Andrews

Lees may well have commissioned this photograph to aid him in the composition of his painting. The central section of *The Golfers* shows virtually the same group of players that appears in the Adamson and Hill photograph, including Allan Robertson, Tom Morris, an unidentified caddy, and Hugh Lyon Playfair. It was Hugh Playfair who, as provost of the then dilapidated town of St Andrews, initiated its radical transformation in the 1840s. The overhaul included the improvement of leisure facilities, and Playfair, a keen golfer, saved the town's golf courses from erosion. Fellow golfer Allan Robertson was a third-generation "featherie," or golf-ball maker, and reputedly the best golfer in St Andrews. His pose has been directly copied onto Charles Lees's painting.

Twentieth Century

The exhibition next focuses on the early years of the twentieth century, beginning with a portrait that celebrates one of Scotland's most endearing golfing legends, Tom Morris, Sr. In September 1902 The Royal and Ancient Golf Club of St Andrews commissioned Sir George Reid to paint a portrait of Tom Morris (plate 19) to mark his dedication and years of service to the Club and to golf in Scotland. The portrait was received with great enthusiasm upon its unveiling to the assembled members at their 1903 spring meeting. Morris was eighty-one years old when the portrait was painted. Born on June 16, 1821, in North Street, St Andrews, he spent most of his life on and around the St Andrews links and was a frequent player in matches there. In 1851 Morris accepted an offer of employment as keeper of the green at Prestwick, on the west coast of Scotland; he spent fourteen years there in that capacity. The Club enticed Morris back to his home city in 1864, employing him as their keeper of the green until 1903. In addition to his duties at the Club, Morris ran a flourishing club- and ball-manufacturing business, designed many golf courses, and was responsible for significant advances in greenkeeping. He was also one of the preeminent golf professionals of his era and won the Open Championship four times between 1861 and 1867. Reid's portrait captures Morris in his autumn years. His tweed outfit is painted in the same natural tones as the landscape in which he stands, presumably on the Old Course, suggesting his oneness with the place. His downcast eyes and modest stance belie his stature as golf's first professional and an icon of the game in Scotland.

Moving into the Roaring Twenties, golfing art is represented by the two Irish artists Sir William Orpen and Sir John Lavery. Both were highly sought-after and fashionable society portraitists who also fulfilled the very different role of official war artists. Orpen's striking full-length portrait of the Prince of Wales (plate 20) is a testament to both the glamour of golf in the early decades of the twentieth century and its broadening appeal outside of Scotland. David, Prince of Wales (1894–1972), later Edward VIII, became captain of The Royal and Ancient Golf Club of St Andrews in 1922. The third royal to captain the Club,

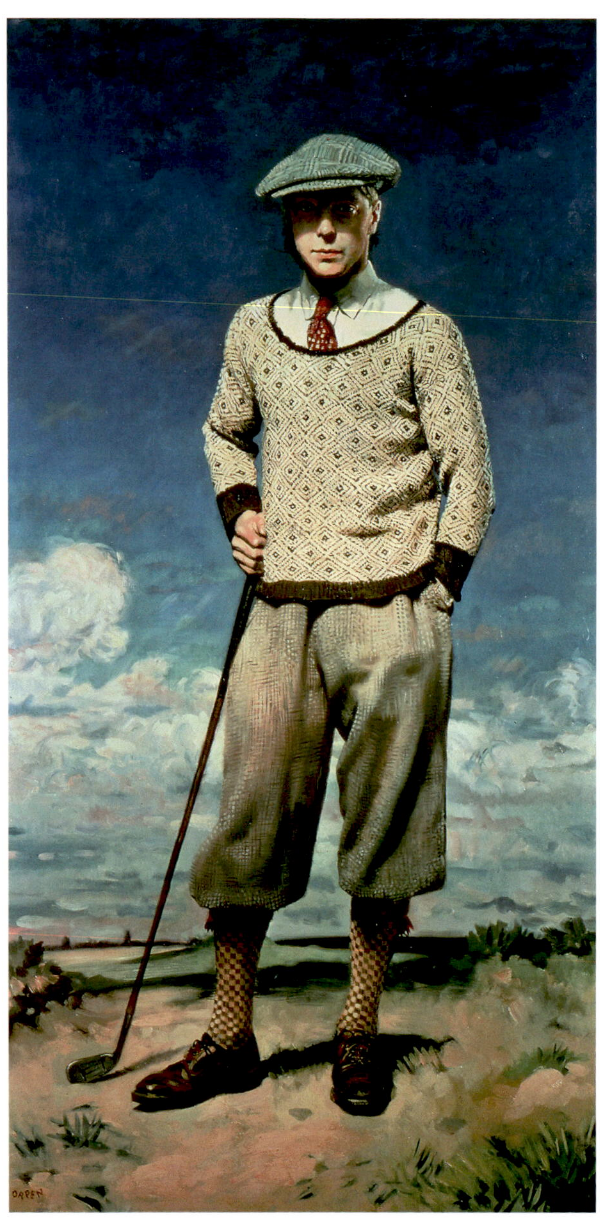

20 SIR WILLIAM ORPEN (IRISH, 1878–1931)

The Prince of Wales, 1927
Oil on canvas, 80 × 40 inches
By kind permission of The Royal and
Ancient Golf Club of St Andrews

the twenty-eight–year-old prince played golf to a fifteen handicap. Predictably, the prince's captaincy created a surge in demand for attendance at the Club's annual ball and medal competitions. On September 27, 1922, approximately 6,000 people gathered to watch the Prince of Wales drive in as captain from the first tee of the Old Course; when he played in the Club's medal competition later in the day, a crowd of around 10,000 was present to watch the popular royal compete.

The Club decided to honor their royal captain by commissioning a portrait of him. Orpen agreed that his fee for the portrait would be "whatever sum was raised amongst the members, but that he hoped it would be in the neighbourhood of £1,000." Appeals for funds were made in 1924 and 1925, by which time the portrait, commissioned in 1922, was still not complete. In November 1925 correspondence between the Club, the artist, and the prince's secretary suggests that the portrait was delayed because of the difficulty Orpen had in arranging sittings with the prince. In 1927 Orpen wrote to the Club to inform them that he was dissatisfied with the portrait. The artist offered either to refund £500, half of the commission fee, or to be given the opportunity to modify the painting until he was satisfied with it. Orpen was asked to continue working on the portrait, and by September 1927 it was finally finished. Although the Club had requested that the prince pose in the traditional red captain's coat, his preference was to be shown wearing a knitted sweater and plus fours, fashionable attire that greatly influenced styles in golfing clothing. Orpen's portrait marks a departure from the stiff and repetitive formality of most official royal portraiture. The fact that the prince asked to be portrayed in golfing attire suggests that the sport afforded him an opportunity to escape the enforced ceremony and crushing formality of his position as future king—a position he relinquished as a result of his controversial abdication in 1936 to marry an American divorcee, Wallis Simpson.

The early 1900s saw golf's popularity spread beyond Scotland's borders. Quick and affordable rail transport encouraged travel in the United Kingdom, ensuring that Scottish golfing centers such as North Berwick and St Andrews teemed with tourists and golfers (plates 21 and 22). The Caledonian Railway Company built the famous Gleneagles Hotel and golf courses, served by their own railway station, to cater to this market.

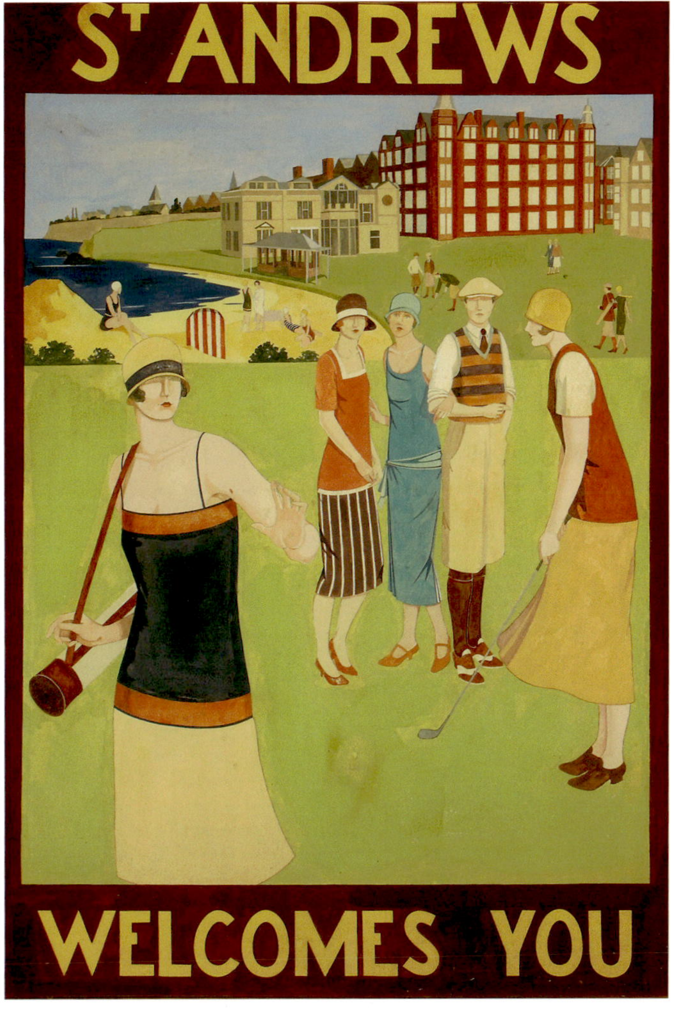
ST ANDREWS
WELCOMES YOU

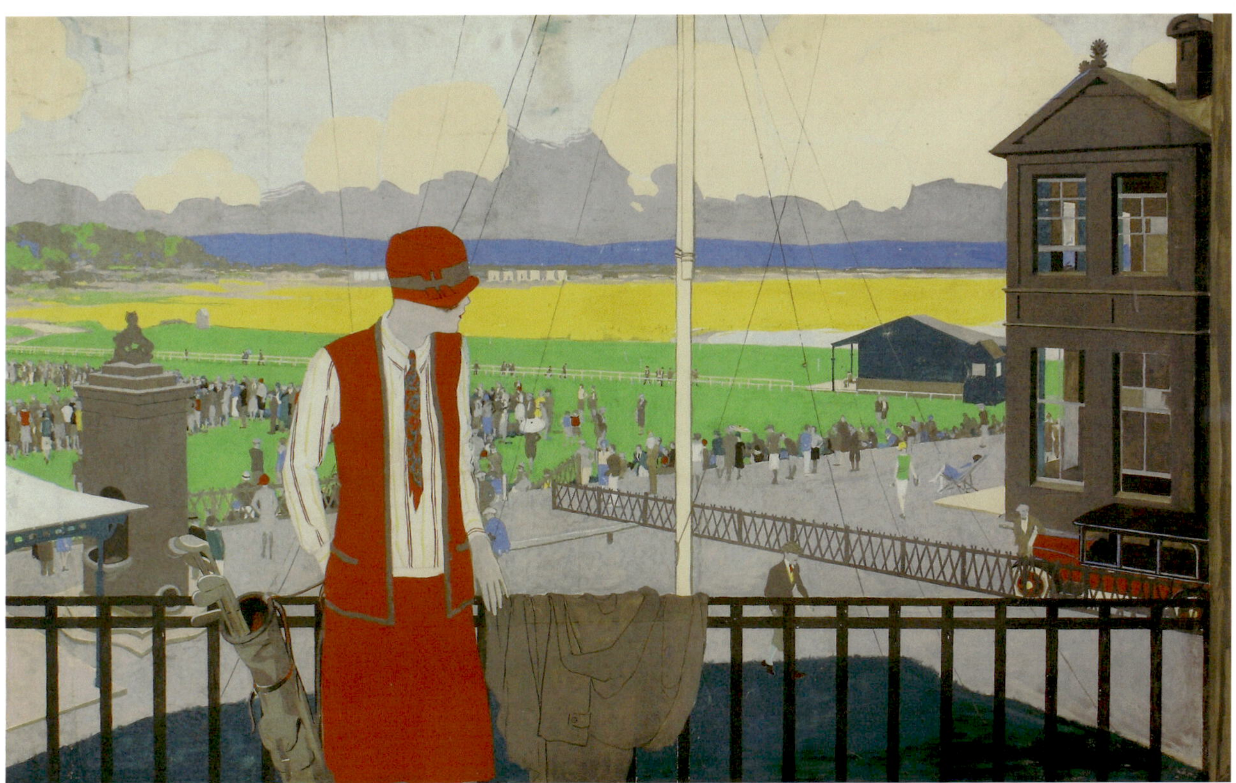

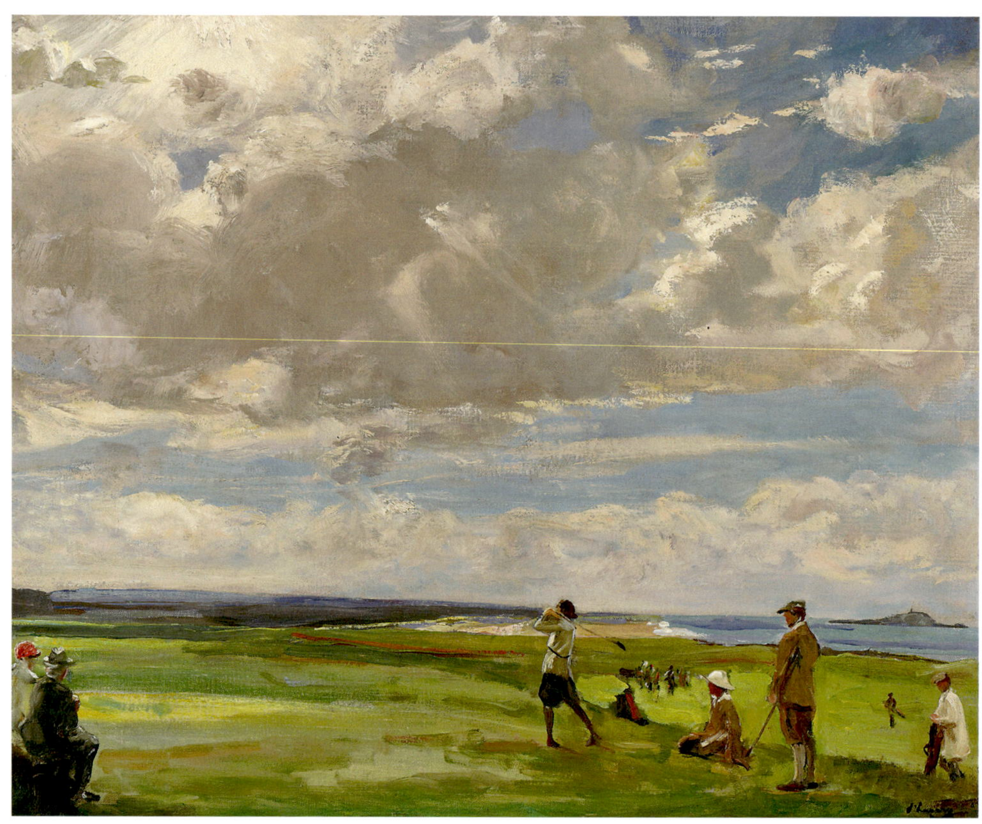

During the 1920s North Berwick had also developed into an extremely fashionable golf destination, as evidenced by the number of grand villas and mansions that were built there. It advertised itself as the "Biarritz of the North." Among the town's visitors were the painter Sir John Lavery and his wife, who between 1919 and 1924 regularly stayed at Westerdunes, the luxurious home of Sir Patrick Ford, a Scottish Unionist Party politician. This location afforded spectacular views directly over North Berwick and across the Firth of Forth, an idyllic and inspiring location for an artist. While visiting the Fords, Lavery painted many landscapes and garden scenes in his characteristic lush and lyrical style. He also painted a series of landscapes featuring the beautifully undulating links with their spectacular coastal views, many of which are peopled with golfers.

One of the most beautiful of these scenes is the painting once incorrectly titled *Lady Astor Playing Golf at North Berwick*, but now known as *Golfing at North Berwick* (plate 23).[11] The mistaken identity of the central female figure is understandable given that Lady Astor was a highly fashionable figure and a very keen golfer. A label revealed on the reverse of the painting, however, lists the true identities of the figures depicted. The young female golfer is actually Alice Trudeau, Lavery's stepdaughter, and the spectators include Alice's mother, Hazel Lavery, who sits by her daughter's side in a white hat; a figure listed merely as "Asquith," which probably refers to Herbert Henry Asquith, First Earl of Oxford, the Prime Minister of the United Kingdom from 1908 to 1916; and Sir Patrick and Lady Ford.

Lavery's characteristic depiction of the luminous sky is particularly arresting (plate 24). In *Golfing at North Berwick*, the artist delights in picking out the dramatic pattern of clouds pierced by rays of sunshine, portrayed with his typical bravura brushwork. The sun's rays rake unevenly over the green, which is depicted with thick slices of green and yellowish paint. Completing her swing, Alice faces toward the sun, which is moving westward, indicating that the game is taking place in the afternoon. Lavery has carefully arranged the figures to emphasize Alice's elegant swing as the picture's highlight. Alice is further indicated as the focus of the painting by the sun's rays, which point directly at her. The painter's stepdaughter is wearing the then-fashionable knee-length skirt, or knickerbockers, with a long "jumper" or cardigan, made popular by Lady Astor. Standing behind her, Sir Patrick Ford is also dressed in knickerbockers, the forerunners of the fuller plus fours, which became fashionable for golfers later in the decade.

Ladies' golf had been popular since the late nineteenth century, when female golfers were compelled by contemporary notions of modesty to struggle in the restrictive full-length skirts, which made little concession to free movement. By 1921, the date of Lavery's painting, the conventions governing female golfing dress had relaxed considerably, with higher hemlines acceptable and the use of the corset and rigid undergarments all but discarded. Young women could enjoy golf without being impeded by their clothes. In fact, the boyish and carefree style of clothing associated with golf became extremely fashionable and was a common subject for French fashion plates in the 1920s and 1930s. Lavery played golf himself, but he candidly admitted that he was not a particularly gifted player. He records that he ". . . once told a Scottish caddie [probably at North Berwick] that I was not much of a golfer and he agreed with me. To the same confession an Irish caddie replied, 'Ah, sir, there are very few men can play like you!'"[12]

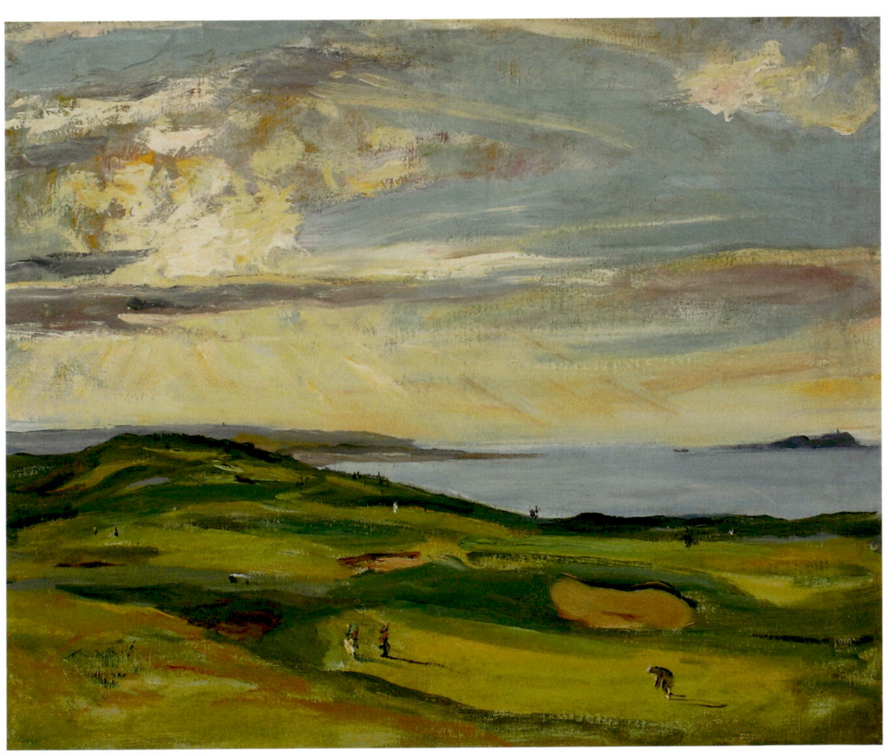

The Golf Course, ca. 1920
Oil on canvas, 36 × 40 inches
United States Golf Association
Museum, Far Hills, New Jersey,
courtesy USGA Museum, 1994-254

For this exhibition, the National Galleries of Scotland commissioned from artist-photographer, biologist, and cultural landscape researcher Patricia Macdonald a group of aerial photographs of Scottish golf courses. Macdonald collaborates with her partner, pilot Angus Macdonald, Professor Emeritus of Architectural Studies at the University of Edinburgh, to produce powerful environmental artworks using aerial photography. The resultant images celebrate and elucidate natural processes, while also documenting and interpreting the effects of human activities—sometimes detrimental, sometimes enhancing—on the land. These commissioned works form part of an ongoing series titled *The Play Grounds*, which depicts the landscapes of leisure activities both historical and contemporary, such as beaches, parks, deer "forests," grouse moors, sports complexes, and urban-fringe shopping malls, among others.

The patterns of bunkers, fairways, and paths, particularly when seen from above, often have the surreal, or "hyper-real," appearance of the alien landscapes of virtual reality. Some ancient Scottish links—based closely on the natural topography of coastal dune systems—have achieved a degree of harmony, both ecological and visual, with the wider landscape within which they are situated, but other courses may contrast uncomfortably with their surroundings, transforming the character of a coastal or rural area. The intensively fertilized emerald swathes of trees, greens, and fairways running between the dark bushes and yellower grass of the rough of the recently constructed courses and clubhouse complex at Archerfield Links, East Lothian (plate 25), are a dramatic example of a hyper-real golfing landscape, which contrasts markedly with the nearby agricultural fields and the remaining original coastal sand dunes.

25 **PATRICIA MACDONALD (SCOTTISH, BORN 1945) WITH
ANGUS MACDONALD (SCOTTISH, BORN 1945)**
*Archerfield Links (the 18th, Dirleton Links Golf Course, and
Clubhouse), East Lothian, 2011*, from *Bunkered Terrain: Golf
Landscapes, Scotland, 2011* (six-part work), part of the
ongoing series *The Play Grounds*, 2011
Photograph, 40 × 26 inches
National Galleries of Scotland, Edinburgh, PGP 809.6

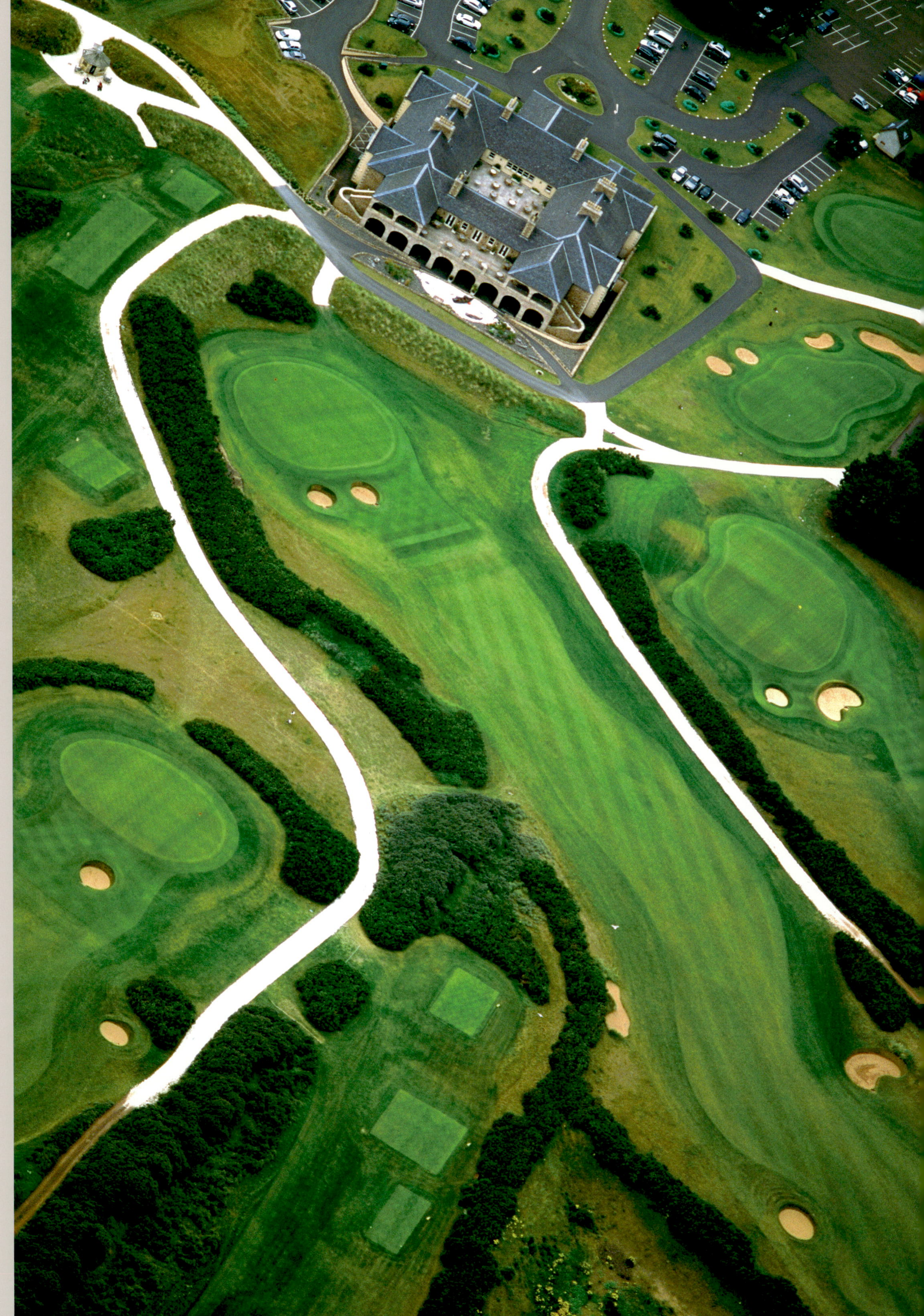

NOTES

1 Act of Parliament of Scotland, March 6, 1457, National Archives of Scotland, PA 5/5, f. 43v. Translated from the original Scots.

2 Act of Parliament of Scotland, May 18, 1491, National Archives of Scotland, PA/2/5. F. 15 or. Translated from the original Scots.

3 D. Robertson, *The South Leith Records* (Edinburgh, 1911), 8.

4 *Diary of Thomas Kincaid, 1687–1688,* (National Library of Scotland, Adv.MS. 32.7.7).

5 Thomas Mathison, *The Goff: An Heroi-Comical Poem in Three Cantos* (1743), in Robert Clark, ed., *Poems on Golf* (Edinburgh: Burgess Golfing Society, 1867), 8.

6 "Act of council and regulations, to be observed by those, who play Yearly for, the City of Edinburgh's Silver Club." Edinburgh Town Council Minutes, Edinburgh City Archives, March 7, 1744, 206–210.

7 Ibid.

8 Quoted in Douglas Guthrie, "The Harveian Tradition in Scotland," in *Journal of the History of Medicine and Allied Science* XII, no. 4 (1957?): 123.

9 George Fullerton Carnegie, "The Golfiad," in Clark, ed., *Poems on Golf*, 22.

10 Quoted in Peter N. Lewis and Angela D. Howe, *The Golfers: The Story Behind the Painting* (Edinburgh: National Galleries of Scotland, 2004), 42.

11 K. McConkey, *Sir John Lavery* (Edinburgh: Canongate Press, 1993), 146.

12 Sir John Lavery, *The Life of a Painter* (New York: Little, Brown and Company, 1940), 183.

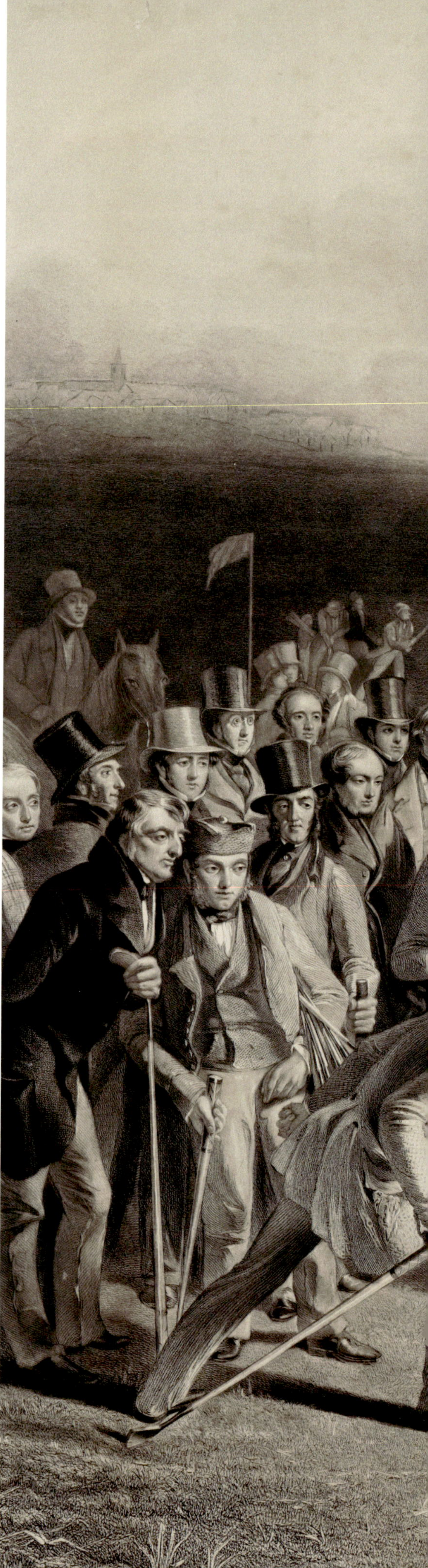

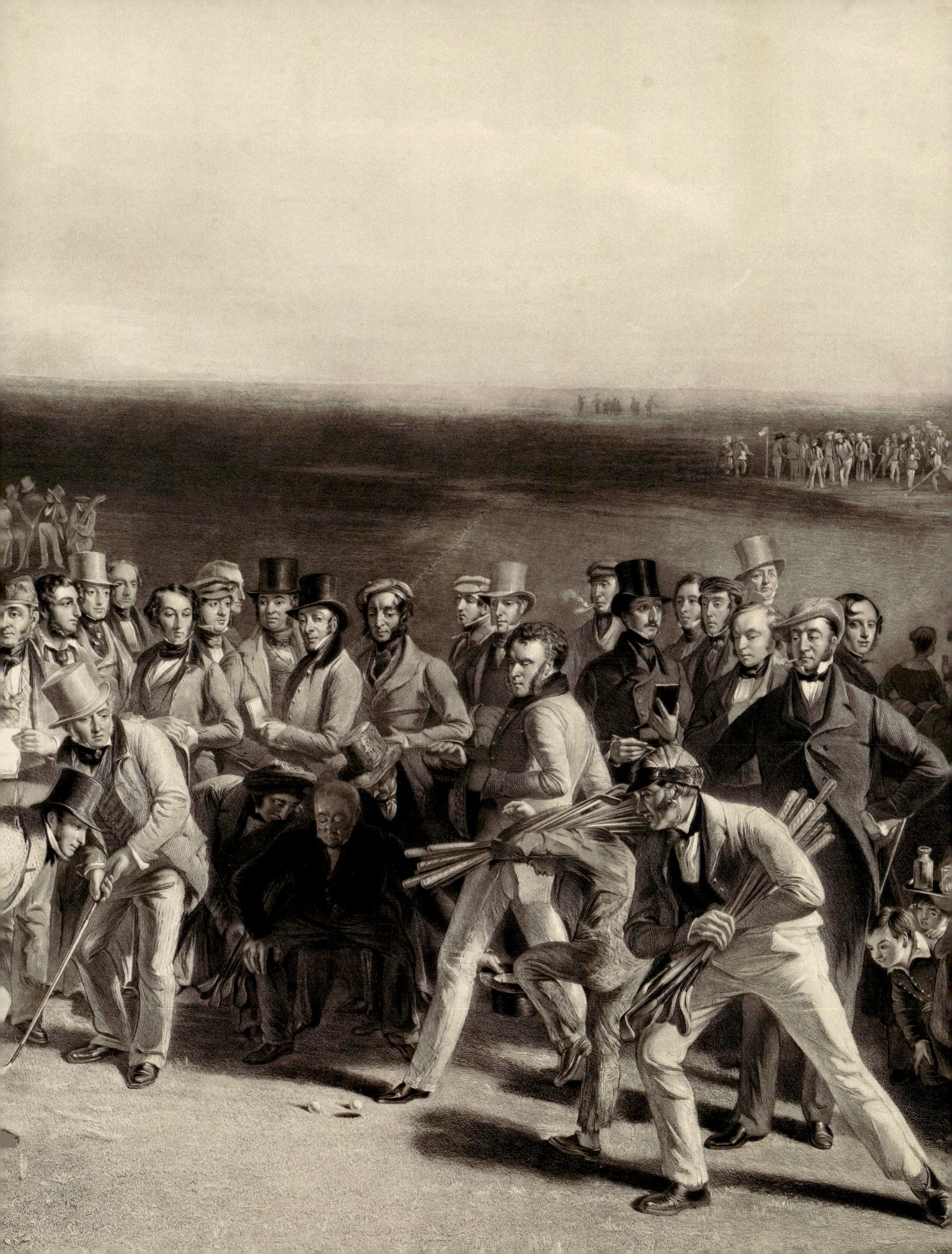

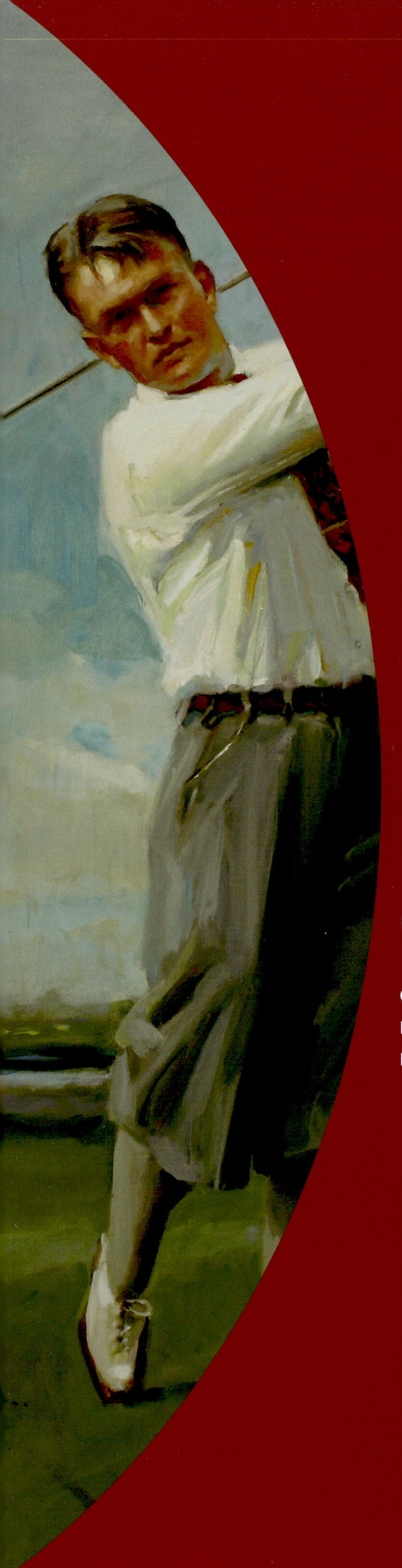

A Game of Considerable Passion

Golf in American Art

CATHERINE M. LEWIS, PH.D.
RICHARD ANTHONY LEWIS, PH.D.
RAND JERRIS, PH.D.

Shipping manifests and estate inventories suggest that golf was played in the Americas as early as the seventeenth century, if only by a very few people. By the end of the eighteenth century early golfing societies such as the South Carolina Golf Club (1786) in Charleston and the Savannah Golf Club (ca. 1794) in Georgia had been organized, although there were no permanent golf courses for these clubs. It is thought that club members simply set up golf holes on public land whenever they wanted to play. During the nineteenth century, players came mostly from the upper echelons of society, and not until the 1890s did the sport begin to become part of the average American's consciousness. The rise of golf at this time was coincident with the reduction in the length of the work week and the rise of middle-class leisure. Golf in America also arose concurrent with suburbanization and the city parks movement. At a cultural level, it provided fatigued city dwellers access to sunlight and fresh air, a necessity advocated by civic leaders and an emerging group of sports enthusiasts across the country.

With its concentration on moderate exercise, skill, and obedience to the rules of fair play, golf appealed to an emerging business-class culture composed of skilled and educated workers. But this new focus on leisure had to overcome traditional Protestant aversions to recreation. In a December 1894 issue of *Harper's Magazine*, Caspar Whitney wrote, "It must be admitted unhesitatingly that we are only just learning how to play, we have not been, nor are we yet, a nation of pleasure seekers. We are a practical people."[2] Within the space of a few years commentators such as Bruno Lasker began stressing the health benefits of the game: "One returns from an afternoon of golf renewed and refreshed," he wrote. "It is suitable for both men and women of all ages. . . . Nothing better could happen than the extension of opportunities for golf to a far larger number of our people." In addition to its healthful benefits, golf was beginning to be viewed in the popular imagination as a sign of material success, and club membership marked social ascendancy.[3]

In 1888 the "Apple Tree Gang," led by Scots John Reid and Robert Lockhart, founded the first modern golf club in the United States, the Saint Andrew's Golf Club in Yonkers, New York.[4] The United States Golf Association (USGA) hosted the first U.S. Open, U.S. Amateur, and U.S. Women's Amateur championships in 1895, the year after it was founded. The game grew quickly in popularity, and artistic representations, paintings, postcards, illustrations, and advertisements in well-known magazines demonstrated the sport's appeal to the growing middle class.[5] By 1896 there were more than eighty courses in the United States; within six years, there were 982.[6] Unlike golf in Scotland, which was largely played on common areas ("linksland") that were open to the public and attracted both titled gentry and working-class men and women, golf in America retained its close connection to the elite and rising middle-class culture.[7] Those who played generally had the resources to seek healthful recreation, often in seaside communities such as Newport or Jekyll Island or mountain resorts such as Lake Placid and Poland Springs, away from the bustle of newly industrialized cities such as New York.

Although there were some exceptional professional players in the early decades of the twentieth century—the majority of whom were Scottish immigrants—amateur golf reigned supreme in America. Professional golfers did not truly gain respectability until the 1920s. Historian Benjamin Rader argued that amateurs imported and wholeheartedly embraced an ethic of amateurism from upper-class English sportsmen, needing no officials to police the rules but instead embracing the tenets of fair play.[8] Golf became the quintessential amateur sport partly because adherence to the rules was the responsibility of the players. This amateur ethic dovetailed with both the pursuit of refined leisure activities and the self-regulation expected in the atomized, industrial economy taking shape among the managerial class during the early twentieth century.

Public parks were also growing in popularity and number at this time, championed by landscape architects such as Frederick Law Olmsted. Like golf courses, parks were designed to provide safe, comfortable spaces for city dwellers to engage in healthy leisure activities. Parks also encouraged social practice characterized by decorum and propriety as well as conspicuous display—themes appropriate for both golf and art. This growing public parks movement and the trends toward health, recreation, manners, and self-betterment further contributed to the popularity of golf in America among men and women both young and old.

Yet golf as a subject has not attracted artists on a grand scale in America in the way that other sports such as skating, horse racing, hunting, and boating have. In Scotland, Charles Lees's *The Golfers* (see plate 14) demonstrates through scale and ambition how deeply the game is embedded in the Scottish national consciousness. No iconic American painting celebrating golf is fixed in the popular imagination in the way that Gilbert Stuart's *The Skater: Portrait of William Grant* (1782; National Gallery of Art, Washington, D.C.) represents ice skating, or Thomas Eakins's *The Champion Single Sculls* (*Max Schmitt in a Single Scull*) (1871; The Metropolitan Museum of Art, New York) celebrates rowing. Golf has provided inspiration for countless illustrators, photographers, and portraitists, but the subject has only occasionally attracted well-known artists.[9] Fine art representations of golf tend to come in clusters of themes and, to a lesser degree, periods. The first significant expression is landscape painting, dating roughly from 1900 through the 1940s. Second, portraits of celebrated figures were popular during the first half of the twentieth century, with a revival of interest in the 1970s. Third, the sport is captured in all manner of popular media, from illustrations such as Norman Rockwell's advertisements of the 1920s (see plate 51) to the stroboscopic photographs of Harold Edgerton (see plates 44–47). Finally, artists have depicted aspects of golf as humorous social commentary, from the gentle irony of Charles Schulz's cartoons (see plate 52) to the sophisticated satire published in *The New Yorker* (see plates 53–56).

The Golfing Landscape

Conceived as a sport for elite and rising middle-class Americans, golf's ascent in the United States paralleled public interest in landscape architecture and painting. With antecedents in the cemetery movement beginning in the 1830s, the late nineteenth-century city parks movement had two primary goals: first, to incorporate the city into a comprehensive plan and, second, to improve the overall physical and mental health of city dwellers. The topography of cities such as Chicago, New York, St. Louis, and Atlanta underwent radical transformation, complete with slum clearing, in the name of sanitation and public health. Following this development, American golf course design began evolving into an art during the early years of the twentieth century. Some of the game's best designers, including Donald Ross and Alister MacKenzie, built their reputations with courses such as Seminole Golf Club in Florida and Oak Hill Country Club in New York (Ross), Cypress Point Club in California, and Augusta National Golf Club in Georgia (MacKenzie).[10] Golf satisfied the need for moderate and wholesome exercise implicit in these manicured and

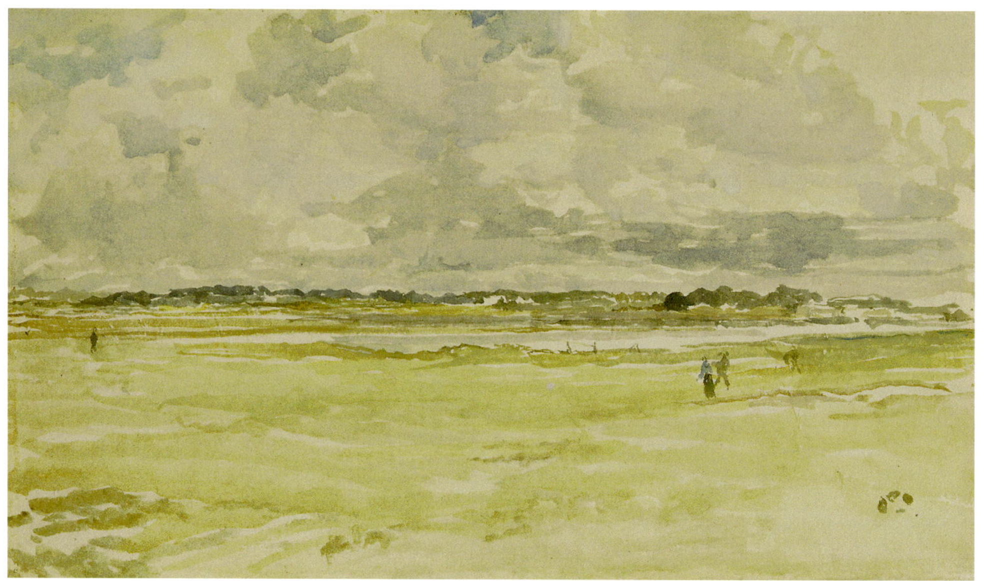

manufactured landscapes, representing a delicate balance of mental and physical ener-gies. But it also provided an opportunity to admire lush scenery, improved by the skill of the resident greenkeeper. Documenting or commemorating this aesthetic experience sud-denly appealed to the new class of artists emerging at this time. Impressionism, with its emphasis on middle-class sociability enacted in suburban landscapes, was a particularly appealing style. Some advanced American artists had absorbed the lessons of Édouard Manet (1832–1883) and Edgar Degas (1834–1917). Perhaps more importantly, the shock value of Impressionism had waned by 1900, making it an appropriate and acceptable style for landscapes in polite society.

Without knowledge of the titles, one would be hard-pressed to identify some of the ear-liest American landscapes as representations of golf. James McNeill Whistler's sketch *Grey and Silver: The Golf Links Dublin* (plate 26) hardly differentiates the figures from the landscape, making it difficult to determine that they are golfers. Best known for his por-traits and nocturnes produced in the 1860s and 1870s, Whistler completed this small study three years before his death.[11] The painting is akin to beach scenes such as *Noc-turne in Black and Gold: Entrance to Southampton Water* (ca. 1872; Art Institute of Chicago, Stickney Fund), which depicts an enormous expanse of atmospheric sky set against a low horizon that is populated with indistinguishable figures. Whistler's sketch is, in many ways, not so much about playing golf as it is about the sport's ability to inspire artistic expression. American by birth, Whistler spent the better part of his career in London, having a profound influence on English art. Other artists, such as Irishman Sir John Lavery (1856–1941), would follow Whistler's format in depicting golf courses. Some early Ameri-can Impressionists followed suit, selecting golf courses as a subject for aesthetic reasons rather than for their associative value, much less for a love of the game. Whistler's title makes clear that this is first and foremost a composition study in gray and silver, yet the painting speaks to the ubiquity of the sport in the United Kingdom.

Landscape painting largely implies sufficient leisure time to see and appreciate beautiful sights as well as some degree of control or stewardship over land reserved purely for aesthetic or physical enjoyment—constructing and maintaining a golf course was, and still is, an expensive proposition. Participation in the sport also implies adequate means to purchase new equipment, fashionable clothing designed for the game, and expensive country club memberships. In short, golf implies a degree of exclusivity. Around this exclusivity is built a network of social relationships that reflects the politics of race and class in American life in the early twentieth century.

Though of humble origins, artist Childe Hassam achieved the stature of a "mammoth" in artistic circles and moved freely in elite society in the Hamptons, Old Lyme, Cos Cob, and Gloucester.[12] He was born in Boston, took lessons at the Boston Arts Club and Lowell Institute, and in 1883 left to study in Paris. He eventually settled in New York and became a leading American Impressionist.[13] Hassam's painting *Dune Hazard, No. 2* (plate 27) likely depicts a course he played often, the Maidstone Club in East Hampton, founded in 1891 and professionally designed by Scottish immigrant Willie Tucker. Hassam was himself a member there, regularly swimming in the pool, playing the course, and documenting his

27 CHILDE HASSAM (AMERICAN, 1859-1935)

Dune Hazard, No. 2, 1922
Oil on canvas, 22 × 44 inches
American Academy of Arts and Letters,
New York

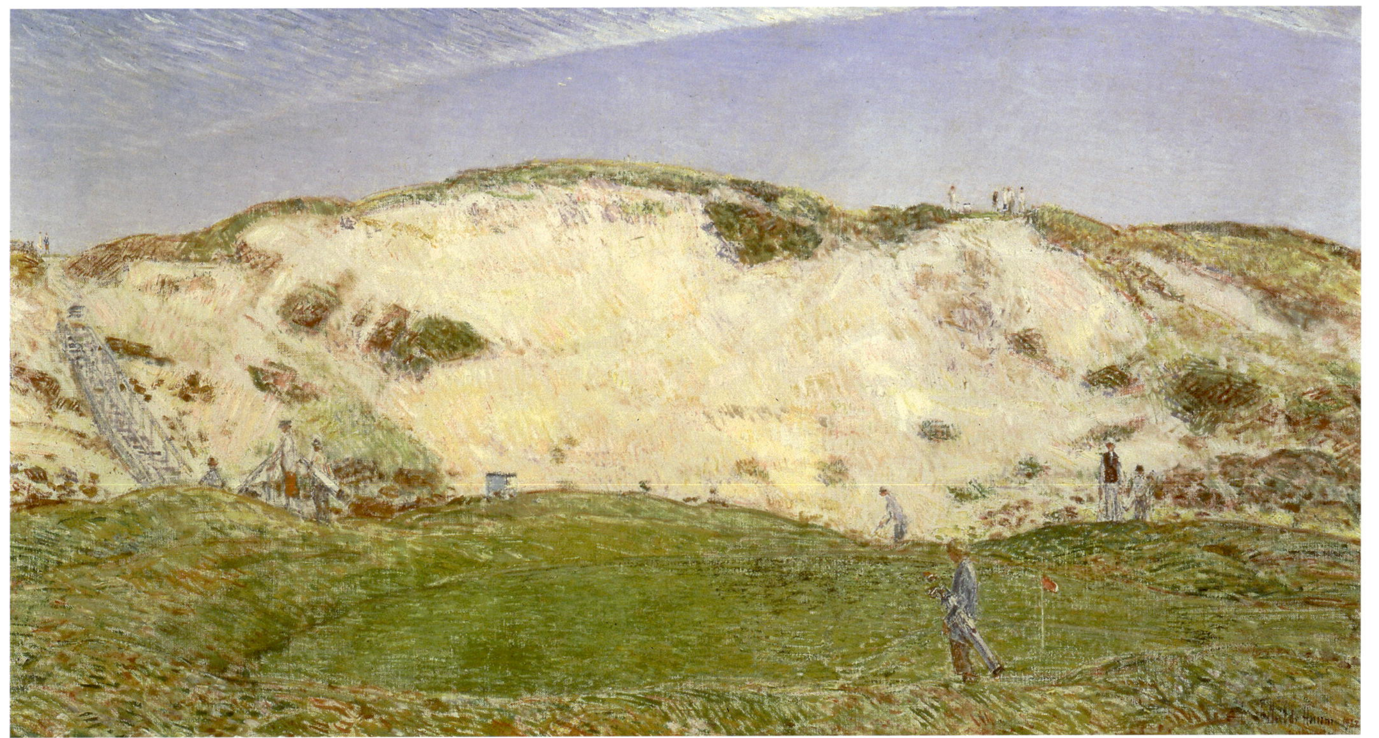

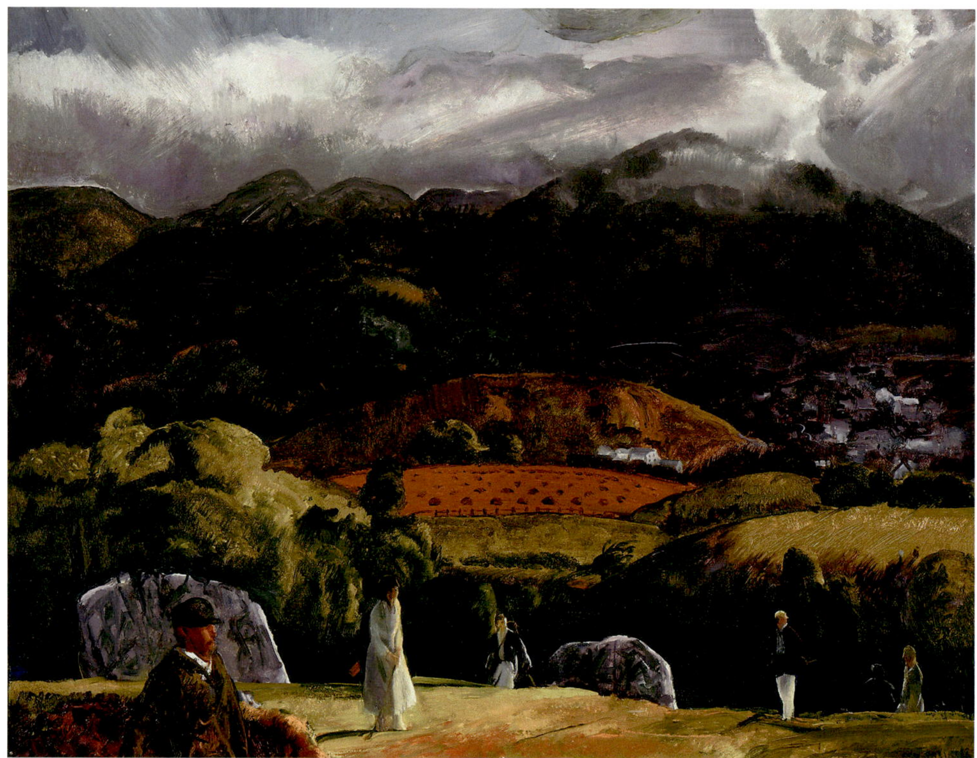

experience in oil and watercolor.[14] Hassam and his wife bought a house on Egypt Lake near the club, and they spent their summers at Maidstone, which he called "a country club discovered by artists."[15]

Like Hassam, George Bellows documented the rise of golf as a social activity in *Golf Course, California* (plate 28), painted six years before Hassam's work. Although there is not much evidence that he played golf, Bellows was an accomplished basketball and baseball player at The Ohio State University. He was talented enough to have been recruited by the Cincinnati Reds, but he enrolled in the New York School of Art instead. Falling in with the circle of Robert Henri, Bellows would later say, "My life began at this point."[16] Like his colleagues—collectively known as "The Eight," including William Glackens, George Luks, and John Sloan—Bellows focused on gritty urban environments. The movement acquired the sobriquet "Ashcan School," a title inspired in part by Bellows's *Disappointments of the Ash Can*, a 1915 illustration for the socialist newspaper *The Masses* that depicts homeless men searching for food.[17] Bellows represented a panorama of urban life, from the most downtrodden to the most privileged. He had rejected the sporting life to become an artist, but his love of sport endured.[18]

Other critics celebrated Bellows's realism, remarking on his "delightfully candid visions" and his ability to present the "raw phenomena of the visible world."[19] *Golf Course, California*, however, is a departure from his typical attention to the lives of the working class. The figures are well dressed and enjoying the leisure that a beautiful and dramatic landscape affords them. The painting reflects a period, beginning in 1916, when Bellows was experimenting with intense, saturated colors and compositions marked for their outstanding

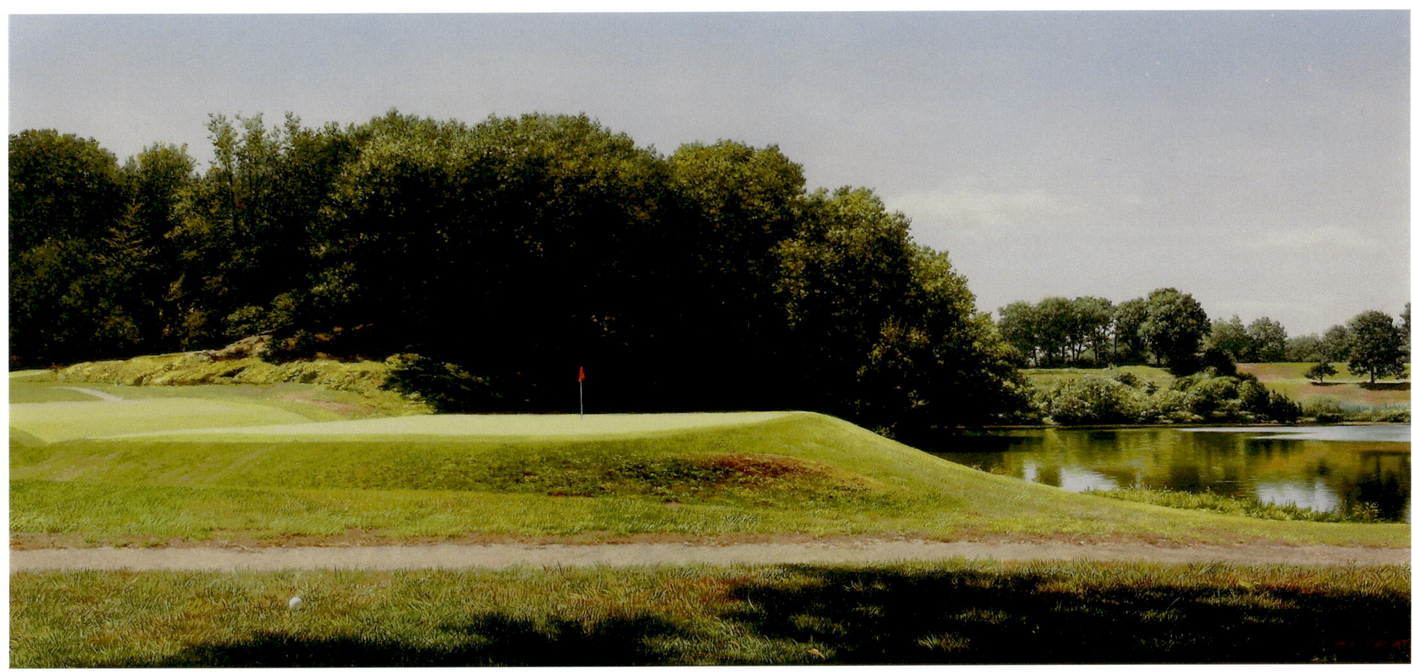

complexity and balance.[20] Art historian Michael Quick argues, "The visual and emotional force of their gorgeous color, which achieves a dazzling opulence exceeded in the work of few American painters of the period, makes the paintings of 1916 and 1917 among the most handsome and enjoyable that Bellows ever produced."[21]

The composition of the foursome in Bellows's work also speaks to the role women played in the sport as well as their growing independence in public life in the late nineteenth and early twentieth centuries. Freed from the strictures that characterized the Victorian era, American women were encouraged to participate in sports such as lawn tennis, archery, golf, and croquet—games that provided moderate exercise but were not too challenging. Such activities blurred the traditional boundaries of the public and private spheres and, in extension, gender lines. Historian George Kirsch argues that in the twentieth century, "The 'athletic girl' had arrived—healthy, lively, energetic, at ease with the new fashions and new sports, and more self-assured, even if she did not have the right to vote or access to the man's realm of business."[22] Modern conceptions of womanhood in this period stood in stark contrast to the Victorian paradigm of the frail feminine constitution.[23] The patina of sportsmanship and character-building associated with judicious exercise, especially the sport of golf, helped alleviate concerns about the propriety of women appearing in the public sphere, where business and pleasure mix. Glenna Collett Vare, a golfing champion who rivaled Bobby Jones as one of the most celebrated and admired American athletes before World War II, became a symbol of this transformation.[24]

Landscape painting in the U.S. waned to a degree after the 1930s but has remained a popular subject in connection with golf. John Falato's *Ninth Hole, Yale University Golf Club* (plate 29) is an excellent example of contemporary landscape painting. In contrast to Bellows, Whistler, and Hassam, who focused on landscapes of courses unrecognizable to the average viewer, Falato highlights a famous hole at the Yale Golf Course, which is regularly ranked as one of the best university courses in the nation. Designed by Charles Blair Macdonald, Seth Raynor, and Charles Banks, the course opened in New Haven in 1926. The course's signature hole, the 213-yard, par-three ninth, is characterized by an unusual sixty-five-yard-deep green—known as a Biarritz green—that has a broad and deep swale separating the front and back.[25] Falato empties the canvas of golfers, thus privileging the landscape over its human inhabitants, much like Whistler's *Grey and Silver* (see plate 26). In contrast to Whistler, there is a sense that Falato has a deep connection to this particular landscape and the associations and meaning behind it.

Like painters, photographers embraced the aesthetics of the golfing landscape. Born in Suchow, China, in 1933, John Yang immigrated with his family first to England in 1937, then to New York City two years later. He began using an Agroflex at the age of thirteen; in 1951 Yang participated in Minor White's summer photography class at the California School of Fine Arts in San Francisco. Despite his love of photography, Yang trained as an architect at the University of Pennsylvania and, after completing his degree in 1957, served with the U.S. Army in Germany. There he bought a German Leica, the finest of the new 35mm cameras. Yang remained in Europe to take photographs after completing his service. Upon returning to New York City he worked as an architect but continued to make photographs inspired by the work of leading modernists Edward Weston, Alfred Stieglitz, Paul Strand, and Robert Frank.[26]

Yang held his first solo exhibition at Norbert Kleber's Underground Gallery in 1965. In 1978 he retired as an architect and turned his full attention to photography. He produced an elegant body of work, including crystalline panoramas of Innisfree Garden in Millbrook, New York; stone faces on New York City building façades; and a large series documenting Mount Zion Cemetery.[27] Yang also photographed golf courses in the Northeast using a Cirkut No. 10. Built in 1903, this spring-powered rotating camera provided a 360-degree exposure. The resulting panoramas have an elegant, lyrical quality that recalls Chinese scroll paintings. The black-and-white panoramas pictured here document some of America's most famous courses: Pine Valley Golf Club, New Jersey (plate 30); Merion Golf Club, Ardmore, Pennsylvania (plate 31); Mill River Club, Oyster Bay, New York (plate 32); and the National Golf Links of America, Southampton, New York (plate 33). Like Whistler and Falato, Yang privileges the landscape. The contours of the bunkers, greens, and fairways—as opposed to figures—provide the central drama. There is a degree of fluctuation between celebrating the courses for their historical associations and presenting them in pure aesthetic terms for the beauty they possess.[28]

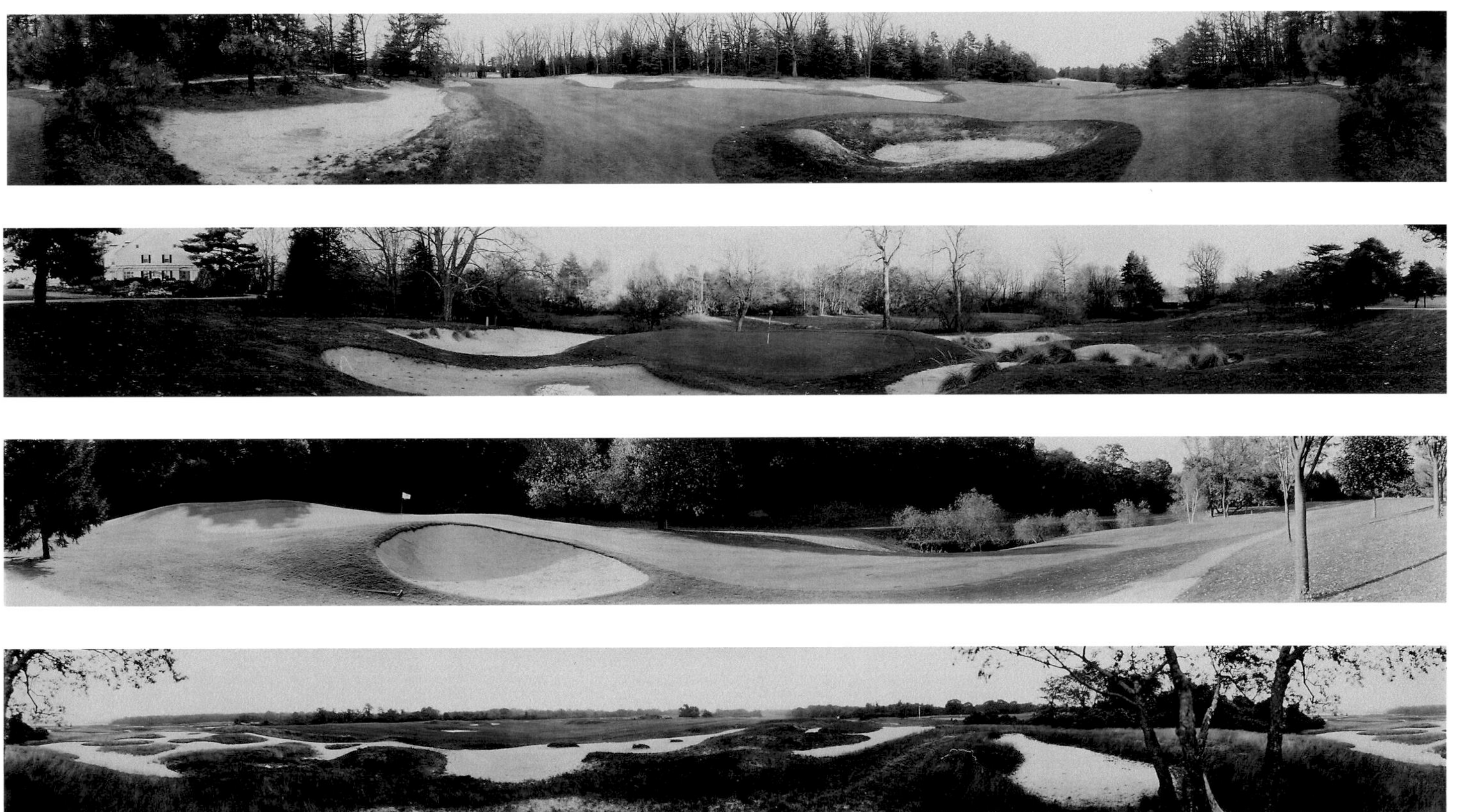

Bobby Jones and the Heroic Portrait

Dutch artists began depicting golfers during the seventeenth century, but portraiture of identifiable golfers was connected most closely with the Scottish tradition. Among the earliest artists to make such portraits was William Mosman, who portrayed the young Sirs James and Alexander Macdonald (of the noted Macdonald Clan from the Isle of Skye) in tartan attire, one holding a wooden golf club and the other a rifle, set in a grove of trees (see plate 8). Later in the eighteenth century, Scottish artist Sir Henry Raeburn painted a number of ambitious portraits of golfers, such as William Inglis, an eighteenth-century surgeon and captain of the Honourable Company of Edinburgh Golfers (see plate 11). Nineteenth-century English and Scottish painting follows this tradition. Golf portraits in the United States, however, did not arise until the twentieth century. Most fall under the category of vernacular illustration—occasionally referred to by the disparaging term "sportrait"—but there are many notable successes. The growth of portraiture in America at this time coincided with the emergence of celebrity culture in the 1920s, with celebrated figures such as Rudolph Valentino and Charles Lindbergh, and the Golden Age of Sports, with legendary athletes such as Babe Ruth and Jack Dempsey.

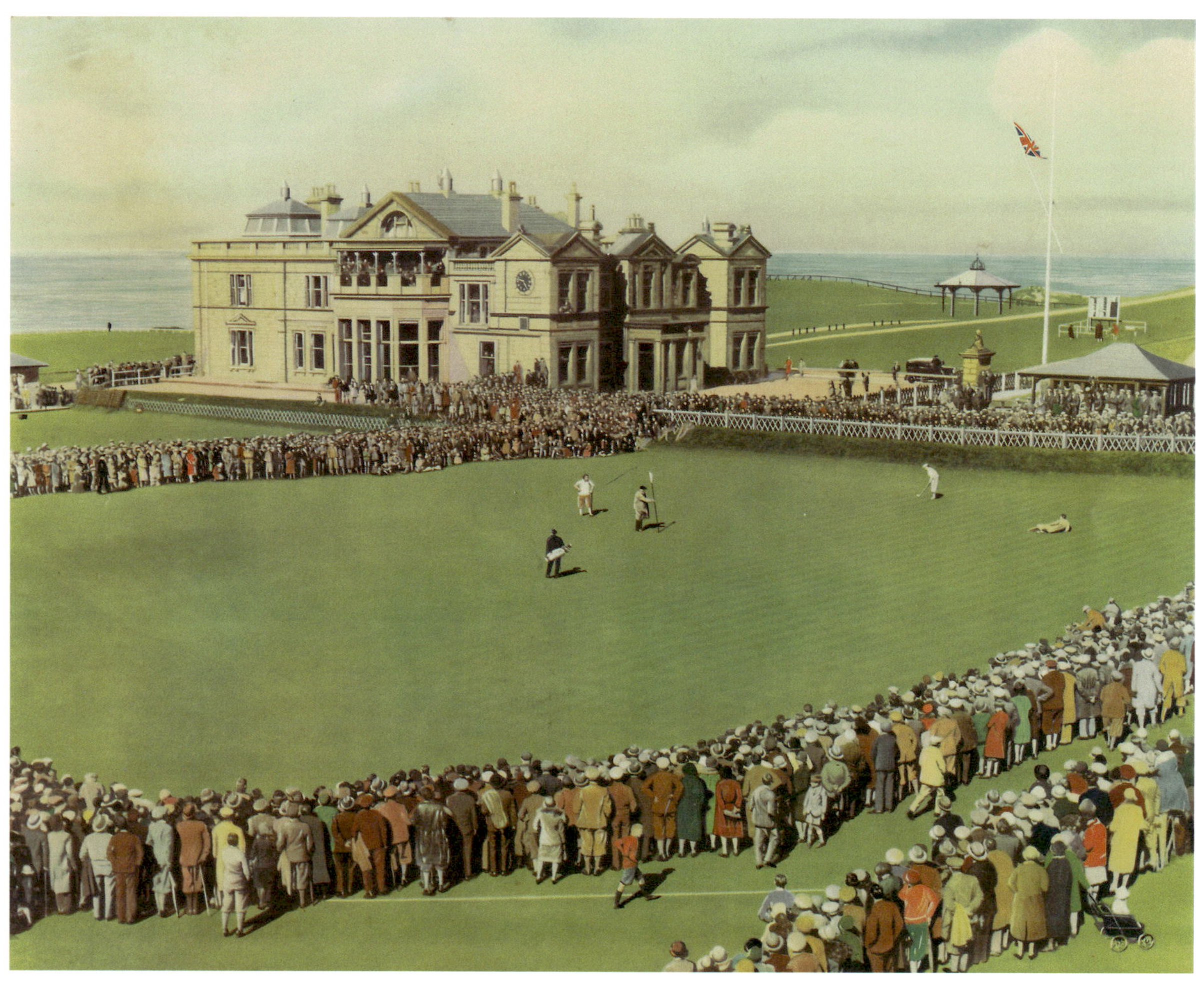

34 UNKNOWN ARTIST

Robert T. Jones Winning the British Amateur at St Andrews, 1930
Lithograph, 11⅛ × 16 inches
Courtesy the Yates Family

None, however, captured the public imagination quite like Robert Tyre "Bobby" Jones, Jr. (plate 34). He popularized golf on an international stage, his sportsmanship called singular attention to the game's best traditions, and his successes both on and off the course inspired generations. In 1930, after a fourteen-year playing career, he became the first and only golfer to win the Grand Slam—golf's four major championships in a single year.[29] In total, Jones played in thirty-one majors and placed first or second more than eighty percent of the time. On November 17, 1930, at the age of twenty-eight, Jones stunned his fans and fellow competitors by announcing his retirement from competitive golf. Over the next thirty years he served as the sport's most famous ambassador; he published books, wrote many newspaper and magazine articles, and signed a contract with Warner Brothers to make *How I Play Golf*, a series of instructional films that were shown in theatres around the nation. He also worked with Clifford Roberts to create and nurture Augusta National Golf Club in Augusta, Georgia, which became the home of the Masters Tournament.

Jones was unique among his fellow Jazz Age celebrities in that he seemed to resist the commodification of his image, even after his retirement and the release of the Warner Brothers series. Many of his contemporaries, notably Walter Hagen, were flamboyant self-promoters who depended more on endorsements and exhibitions than on formal competitions for their livelihoods.[30] While details of Babe Ruth's womanizing or the

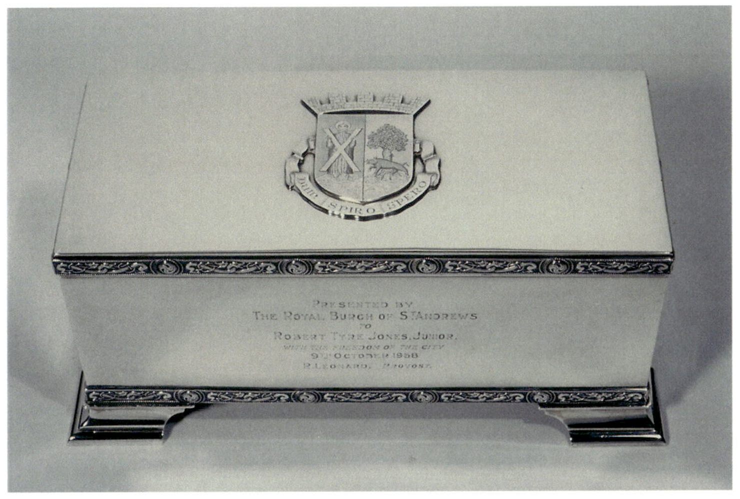

35 UNKNOWN MAKER

*Silver Casket, Freedom of the City of
St Andrews*, 1958
Silver, 4¾ × 10½ × 5¼ inches
Courtesy of the Atlanta History Center,
Atlanta

kidnapping of Lindbergh's son were splashed on the front page of newspapers around the world, Jones's actions on the golf course exuded humility, grace, class, and heroism. He also served as a bridge between America and Scotland—an ambassador of sorts, beloved by both countries for his dedication, integrity, and passion. This love was best illustrated in 1958, when the citizens of St Andrews, Scotland, awarded Jones the Freedom of the City (plate 35), only the second American to be so honored, after Benjamin Franklin 199 years earlier.

It is no surprise that portraitists on both sides of the Atlantic were drawn to Jones as a subject—he represented something more than a heroic athlete. As early as 1923 and especially after he won the Grand Slam in 1930, Jones's effigy was eagerly sought by golf and country clubs. Across the United States and abroad, clubs wished to be associated with his example. Portraitists drew on the Scottish tradition of depicting leading golfers dressed elegantly, establishing a connection to a tradition shrouded in honor. Patrons often insisted that portraits of Jones should serve as testament not necessarily to his skill as a golfer, but to his dignity as a sportsman.

In 1926 a group of prominent Atlanta businessmen commissioned Wayman Adams to commemorate Jones after he won "The Double"—the U.S. Open and the British Open. From the collection of the Atlanta Athletic Club, Jones's home club, the portrait (plate 36) was paid for by subscription to the *Atlanta Georgian* and the *Sunday American* and presented to Jones. Adams was a logical choice for the commission; born in Muncie, Indiana, he studied at the John Herron Art Institute in Indianapolis and was singled out as an astonishing talent before he was twenty years old. In 1910 he accompanied William Merritt Chase on a trip to Italy and two years later traveled to Spain with Robert Henri. Adams had been selected as one of "twelve eminent portrait painters

36 WAYMAN ADAMS (AMERICAN, 1883–1959)

Bobby Jones, 1926
Oil on canvas, 80 × 47 inches
Courtesy Atlanta Athletic Club, John's Creek

of American birth" commissioned to paint some of the heroes of World War I. Relocating to New York City, he counted Calvin Coolidge, Warren G. Harding, and Alice Longworth Roosevelt among his famous clients.

One of the Atlanta businessmen, J. J. Haverty, founder of Haverty's Furniture, insisted that the artist concentrate on Jones's moral and mental abilities rather than his physical prowess. In a letter to Adams dated August 19, 1926, Haverty wrote the following:

> I wish to respectfully suggest further, that in composing the portrait certain things appropriate to the person and conditions should be considered. First—Bobby Jones is not a sport, but a sportsman. He is not in the category of the prize fighter or other athletes whose reputations depend upon their physical skill or animal instincts, and who, like the Mule, have no "pride of ancestry nor hope of prosperity." Bobby Jones's victories in golf are not the result of special physical conditions or accomplishments, but are due to a high order of mental capacity, concentration, and self-control, supported by youthful enthusiasm, great determination, superb ambition, and modesty of demeanor. His life work is not that of a golf player. His mental qualifications and inclinations direct him to the law, and he will enter college next month to study law, with the intention of making it his life work. Golf hereafter with him will be only a plaything, and yet today he is the greatest golfer in the world, because of his antecedents, his blood, and his youthful, praiseworthy ambition. Success has not spoiled him; he is as modest today and as unassuming as he was when a boy of twelve. His future may mean a political career, and I submit that his portrait should be composed with the thought in mind that you are not making the portrait of sport, but of a young man with a high order of mental capacity, of wonderful concentration, self-control, culture, determination, and ambition. Then you will have a portrait that will do justice to him and to you—that will in no sense suggest a funny picture or a caricature of the man or the land in which he lives.[31]

Adams's style echoes Chase's fluid brushwork but also has a penetrating quality from the strain of urban social realism advocated by Henri. Ironically, the focus on Jones's superior ancestry contrasts Adams's own upbringing. The son of a farmer, he first gained attention for his artistic talent at the Indiana State Fair. It is perhaps for this reason that Haverty repeatedly stressed that Jones was no "sport," but rather an honest and admirable sportsman. Adams was a dazzling portraitist, capturing the essence of his sitters' personalities through bravura paint handling that was just modern enough for the opinion leaders' tastes—a perfect embodiment of the reflected late nineteenth-century European modernism expected by astute businessmen such as Haverty and members of the Atlanta Athletic Club.

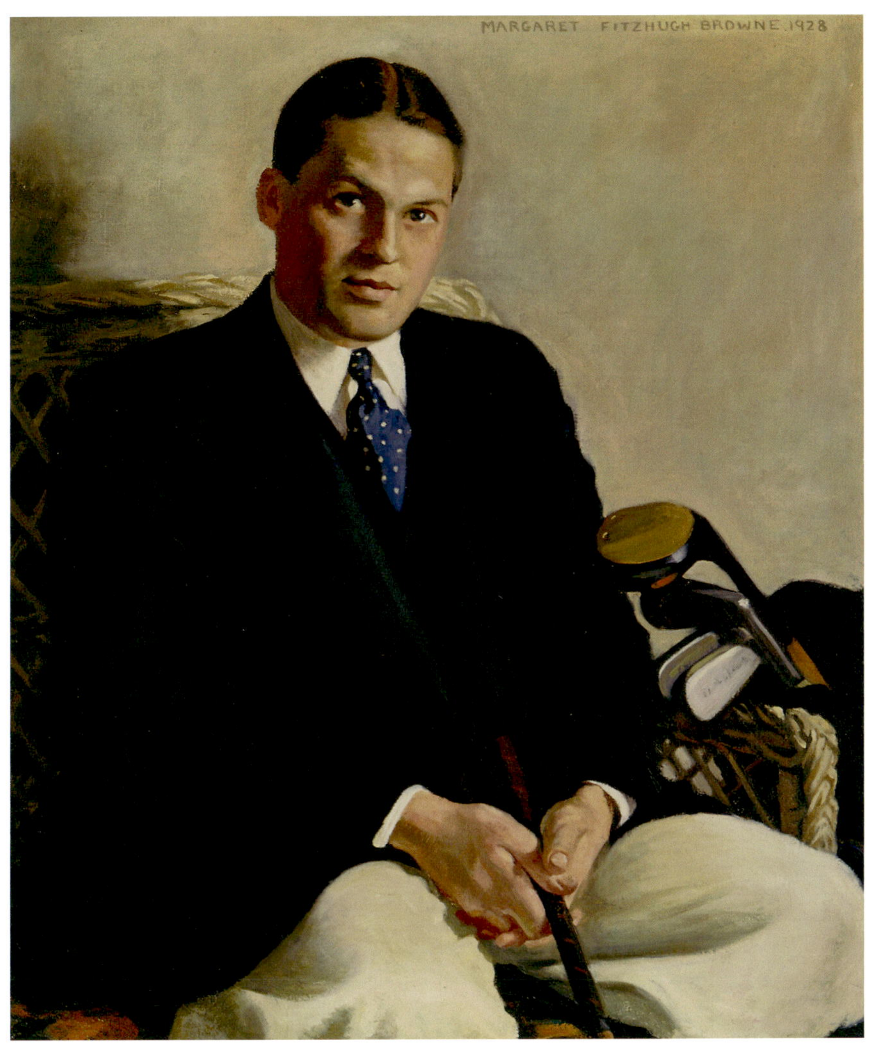

In the interim, between Adams's portrait and Jones winning the Grand Slam, Boston artist Margaret Fitzhugh Browne completed a portrait of Jones (plate 37). Browne was influenced by Joseph DeCamp, one of her teachers at the Massachusetts Normal School. Later mentored by Edmund Tarbell and Frank Benson at the School of the Museum of Fine Arts, Boston (1910–1911), she also enjoyed private instruction from Albert Munsell and Richard Andrew. In addition to painting, Browne served as the art editor of the *Boston Evening Transcript* from 1919 to 1920 and published the book *Portrait Painting* in 1913. She became known for her portraits, still lifes, and domestic scenes. Following a medieval conceit, Browne often depicted in her portraits an attribute illuminative of some aspect of the sitter's personality. For Bobby Jones, she included his personal playing set of hickory-shafted golf clubs.

37 **MARGARET FITZHUGH BROWNE**
(AMERICAN, 1884–1972)

Portrait of Bobby Jones, 1928
Oil on canvas, 37 × 31 inches
High Museum of Art, Atlanta, 28.26

Portraits of Jones answered the need for images of the modern heroic American type, accomplished in both physical and mental arenas. Unlike Haverty's vision of the ill-bred, animalistic, and likely foreign "sport," Jones is described as not seeking fame and fortune through his athletic ability, but as a gentleman who had a higher calling—the law, or possibly even a political career. Descriptions of his modesty suggest a likening to the myth of Cincinnatus, the ideal of the selfless, altruistic statesman who voluntarily surrenders power when he could easily retain and increase it—an image so expertly crafted by George Washington's followers. Here was a man due all spoils and glory who chose to relinquish it in the name of civic virtue, devotion to community, and domestic comfort.

Based on a photograph taken by *Atlanta Journal* sportswriter O. B. Keeler, William Steene's portrait of Jones—sometimes referred to as *The Last Look*—captures something of this quality (plate 38). Jones is relaxed, yet focused. His stance suggests a momentary interruption, presenting his cool, steely gaze, estimating the distance for what is perhaps a chip shot. Although he is neatly dressed, Jones's tousled hair and rumpled clothes also convey his sense of ease as he faces a monumental challenge—winning the Grand Slam. We see him at the exact moment that he becomes not only the world's most talented and famous amateur, but the undisputed finest golfer in the world. His cool confidence and gentlemanly bearing were meant as example, just as George Washington appeared as a picture of humble resolve and supreme self-confidence in portraits by Gilbert Stuart and Rembrandt Peale.

There is, however, an inherent conflict at the heart of the myth of Cincinnatus. One cannot get power by giving it away unless one possesses power in the first place, and it is clear that Jones recognized that his refusal to turn professional despite many lucrative offers would be interpreted as confirmation of his implacable character. The problem is that Cincinnatus cannot have it both ways. Jones readily participated in the marketing of his own image, acutely aware of the

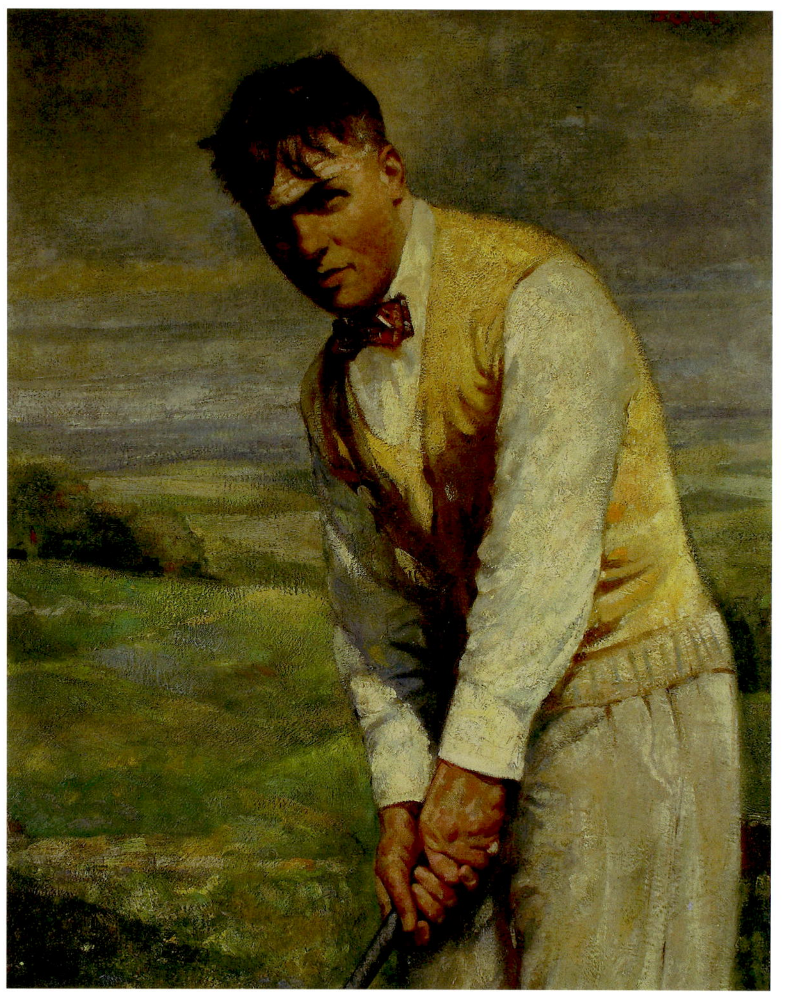

effect that a commissioned portrait would have on his fame. Whether he intended to or not, Jones would profit from golf, not only directly but through association with the tight-knit network of clubs across the country, in political circles, in Hollywood, and through his own law practice. His association with golf and the golf industry provided income and kept him in the limelight. For example, with some training in mechanical engineering, Jones helped design a set of clubs for A. G. Spalding and Bros. It is indeed difficult to conceive of Jones the man as separate from his identity as a famed golf talent. Put another way, a portrait of Jones in his capacity as a lawyer—his avowed interest and identity—would garner only minimal public interest.

However, unlike many celebrities offered the opportunity to capitalize on their fame with a naked ambition, Jones resisted many entreaties. He retained a strong sense of civic responsibility throughout his career and seems to have done his best to negotiate and mediate the conditions of his fame. There was an expectation that what Haverty and his peers wanted in an American hero—a representation of the "wonderful concentration,

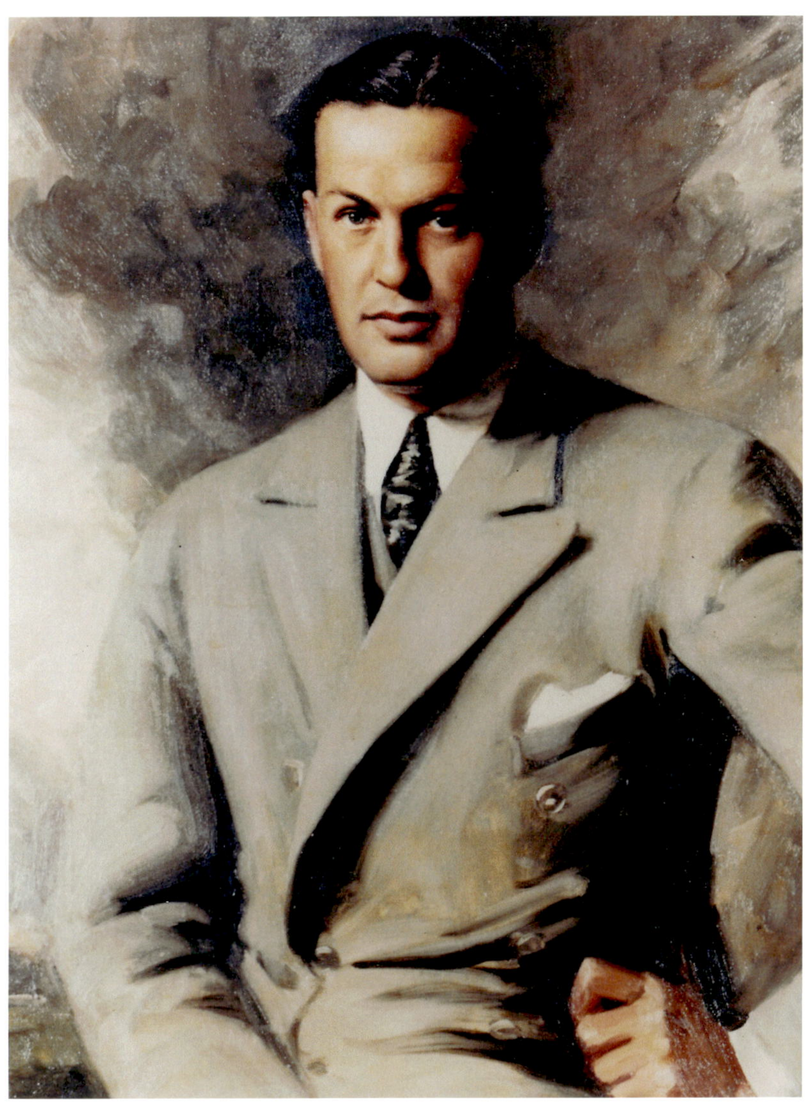

self-control, culture, determination, and ambition"—was becoming an aspiration characteristic of Americans in general. Jones reinforced this combination of modesty and confidence in the Warner Brothers film series. Designed to appeal to the amateur, Jones's films are highly informative and stress the fundamentals, while also conveying a lighthearted sense of camaraderie.

In contrast to the aforementioned portraits, John A. A. Berrie's depiction of Jones (plate 39) seems on the surface to be far removed from the game of golf but best illustrates Jones's signature combination of modesty and confidence. Upon Jones's winning the British Open at Royal Liverpool in Hoylake, England, Sir Ernest Royden commissioned John A. A. Berrie to paint Jones's portrait. Royden, a former captain at Wallasey, later presented the portrait to Wallasey Golf Club, located a few miles from Royal Liverpool, where Jones played qualifying rounds before winning the Open by two shots. Jones described the session with the artist: "Mr. Berrie kept me occupied for no more than thirty minutes and during that time pleasantly refreshed me with a whisky and soda. As an object lesson in painless portraiture, this was the best I have ever seen."[32] Jones was delighted with

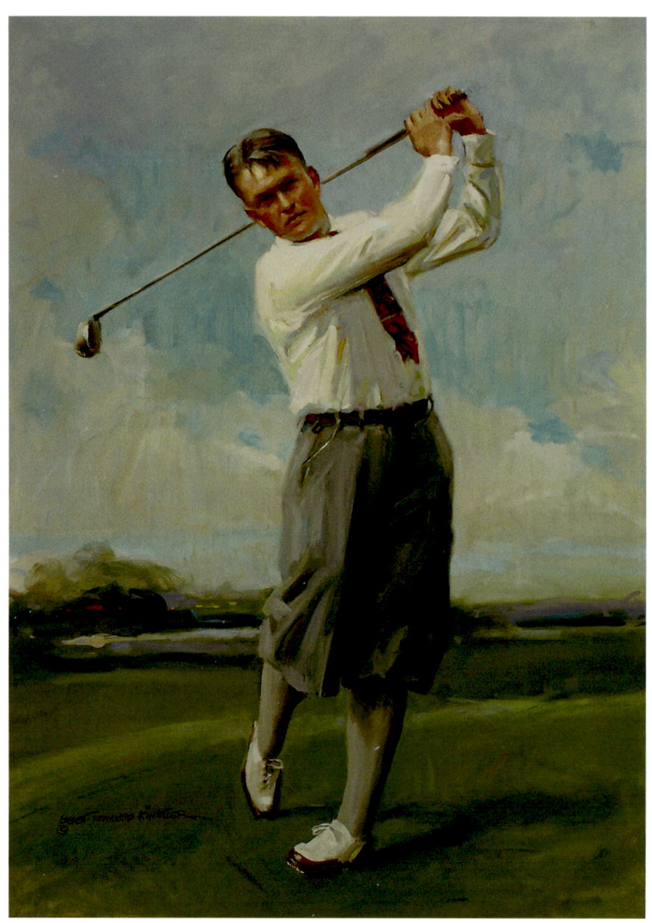

the finished portrait and asked the artist to paint several others of him in different clothes, including the brown suit shown here, and gave them to other clubs, including Royal Lytham and St. Annes in England and Augusta National Golf Club and the Atlanta History Center in Georgia. The latter, shown here, was the only one owned by Jones and was given by his wife Mary to the Atlanta History Center after his death in 1971. It is the centerpiece of the History Center's award-winning exhibition *Down the Fairway with Bobby Jones*, the largest permanent exhibition on Jones in the world.

While a number of portraits of Jones were painted during his competitive career, more recent artists embraced him as a subject long after his heroic deeds were making headlines. New generations are constantly reintroduced to Jones through multiple outlets. Museums—notably the Atlanta History Center, the USGA Museum in Far Hills, New Jersey, and the World Golf Hall of Fame in St. Augustine, Florida—have played an important role in preserving Jones's legacy through permanent and temporary exhibitions. Additionally, he has been the subject of numerous books, articles, newsreels, and feature films. In the past decade, interest in his life and legacy

**40 EVERETT RAYMOND KINSTLER
(AMERICAN, BORN 1926)**

Bobby Jones, 1996
Oil on canvas, 42 × 56 inches
United States Golf Association
Museum, Far Hills, New Jersey,
courtesy USGA Museum, 1996-133

has blossomed, and dozens of writers and historians have published books analyzing his role in the history of sports. Two feature films have included Jones as a character: *The Legend of Bagger Vance* (2000) and *Bobby Jones: Stroke of Genius* (2004). Each spring, his story is retold during the CBS broadcast of the Masters Tournament. His legacy and brand continue to grow with each passing year. Reflecting on the Golden Age of Sports, there are no figures from this era who have been as memorialized or admired as Jones. There is no Babe Ruth scholarship, no feature film about Bill Tilden, and no permanent exhibition on Red Grange. This does not diminish their accomplishments; it simply suggests that Jones's legacy has a kind of currency that is still meaningful and valuable for contemporary audiences. Everett Raymond Kinstler's 1996 portrait of Jones supports this assertion (plate 40). Kinstler specializes in depicting cultural luminaries such as Katharine Hepburn, Tennessee Williams, Lady Bird Johnson, Ronald Reagan, and Tony Bennett, and his work on Jones indicates that the iconic golfer's brand shows no sign of fading.

The sheer number of portraits of Jones should not suggest that no other golfers are represented in American art; in fact, golf changed dramatically after Jones's retirement and World War II. Professional players were once treated as second-class citizens in the sport, with sharp distinction made by tournament organizers between amateurs as "gentlemen" and professionals as "players." Many of the professional players were immigrants (Tommy Armour) or from working-class backgrounds (Walter Hagen), not the elite members of society so prized by the country club set.[33] Prior to World War II, because tournaments rarely had large purses, professional players struggled to supplement their incomes with endorsements and lucrative exhibition matches. After the war and with the advent of television, expanded revenues for professionals relegated amateur golf largely to club tournaments. A new breed of golfer had emerged, epitomized by Arnold Palmer, the public face of golf in the postwar era. He was soon joined by Jack Nicklaus, and their celebrity was on par with movie stars. Along with Jones and later Tiger Woods, these four men dominated golf in America in the twentieth century. American portraiture also underwent a drastic transformation during this period, led by modernist and especially Pop artists such as Andy Warhol. The formality of the earlier era had passed, and new forms of representation reflecting relaxed social mores were emerging.

The early twentieth-century American portraits of Jones depict him as a gentleman, imbued with the grace and privilege of country club life. Combining modeling similar to that of Paul Cézanne and Expressionist color harmonies with the traditional full-length portrait format, Yasuo Kuniyoshi's *Self-Portrait as a Golf Player* (plate 41) offers a bridge between two traditions. On one hand, it is connected to Adams's emphasis on conveying character and likeness, and on the other to the late-modernist obsession with popular, commercial, and celebrity culture, embraced by artists such as Andy Warhol and Larry Rivers. Kuniyoshi also presents the uncommon perspective of an Asian immigrant, who in the 1920s would have largely been excluded from country club life or professional and amateur golf associations by either law or custom. Kuniyoshi came to the United States from Japan in 1906, studied art at night, and in 1910 moved to New York and studied with Robert Henri at the National Academy and the Independent School.[34] By the 1920s he had both the funds and the reputation as an artist to take up golf. More importantly, he conceived of himself as a fashionable golfer in self-portrait.[35] According to Donald G. Goodall, Kuniyoshi

> stands, frontally posed, his attribute in the form of a driver held to his left as an imperial instrument and the various aspects of the golf course precisely and decoratively described in descending scale behind him. Each angled plane within the figure is adjusted to fancifully conceived contours, removing the golfer from reality to the higher estate of symbolic sportsman.[36]

Kuniyoshi's portrait serves as a transitional piece, anticipating a new era in golf art. Bobby Jones and other amateurs dominated the prewar period, and the paintings of that era

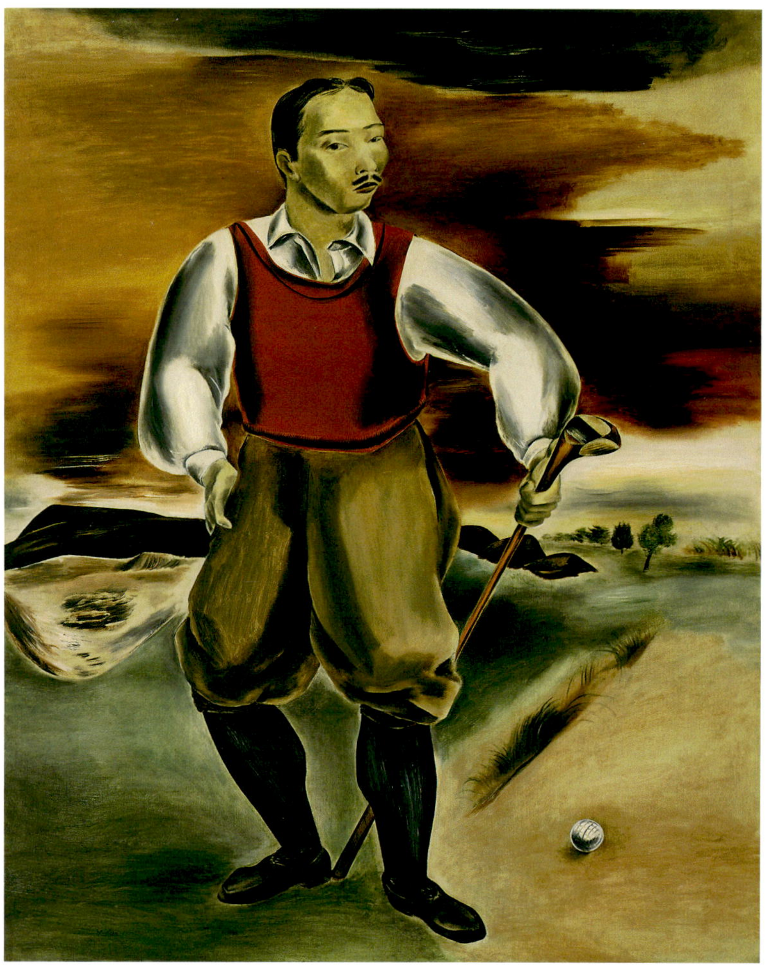

were a fairly conservative echo of avant-garde European practice, including Impressionism and Realism. The sort of men and women who enjoyed amateur golf was the same, from the vantage of class, who collected modern landscape painting—both sport and representation reflected similar values and aspirations. Beginning in the 1930s, when the infrastructure of American public golf was built by President Franklin D. Roosevelt's New Deal agencies, but especially after World War II, golf was changed fundamentally into a middle-class sport. With this, the taste for European-inspired landscape gave way to more popular expressions —Norman Rockwell's drawings, *Peanuts* cartoons, and so forth. The commercial success of the game and its growing celebrity culture sparked a renewed interest in portraiture, together with illustration and social commentary. Golf emerged from the war as big business, spurred by television revenues that increased prize money for competitions and new technologies that altered equipment, style of play, and golf course design. Dozens of golfers emerged in this era as widely recognized, highly paid celebrities.

Golfers' celebrity status particularly appealed to Andy Warhol, who focused on everyday commercial objects—the iconic Campbell's Soup can, dollar bills, or Coca-Cola bottles—as well as popular culture icons such as Marilyn Monroe, Elizabeth Taylor, Mick Jagger, and Jack Nicklaus (plate 42). Warhol simultaneously critiqued and celebrated America's commercial culture.[37] He reflected a postwar cynicism, a concern that the era was "relatively devoid of intellectual and spiritual values," and his many utterances were mundane and tinged with ennui or absurdity.[38] To offer a comparison in the world of sports, one need look no further than Yogi Berra, who famously said, "Baseball is ninety percent mental and the other half is physical." Of Picasso's masterpieces, Warhol flippantly said, "Gee, I could do that in a day."[39] But his famed silkscreened images were mass-produced with liberal use of assistants at his aptly named studio, the Factory. Given the flippancy of Warhol's remark, it is ironic that his canvases regularly rival Picasso's for top price at auctions at Christie's and Sotheby's.

Warhol's art appealed to the titans of American commerce, even as he leveled a critique of the concepts of money, power, and status. Investment banker and art collector

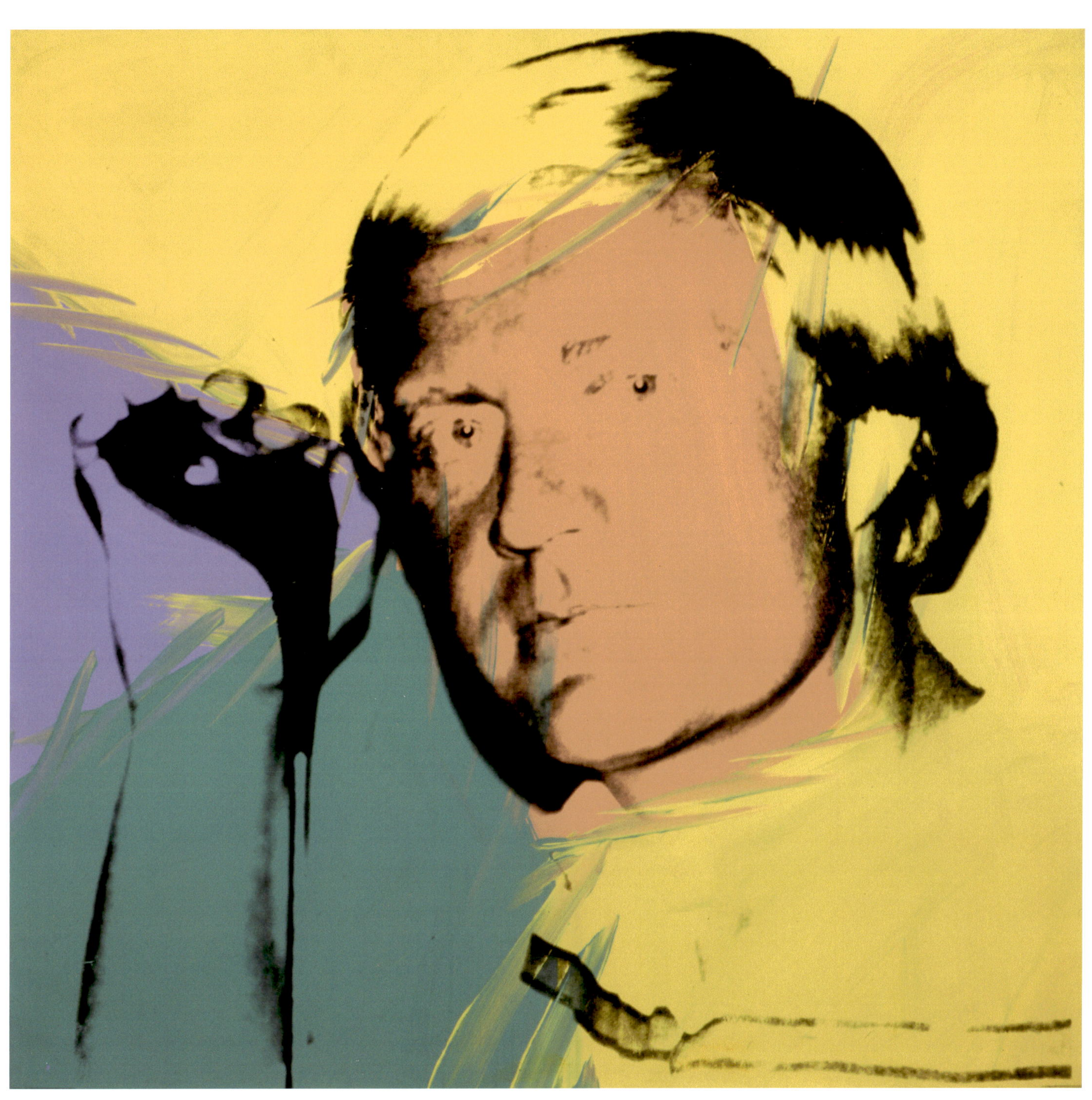

42 **ANDY WARHOL (AMERICAN, 1928–1987)**

Jack Nicklaus, 1977
Acrylic and silkscreen ink on linen, 40 × 40 inches
The Andy Warhol Museum, Pittsburgh, Founding
Collection, Contribution The Andy Warhol Foundation
for the Visual Arts, Inc., 1998.1.702

Richard Weisman commissioned Warhol for $800,000 to create a series depicting famous athletes, including Muhammad Ali, Pelé, Chris Evert, Dorothy Hamill, and Jack Nicklaus. The artist elected not to present them as exemplars of enduring American values, but rather as dynamic celebrity brands to be marketed and consumed by an eager public. It comes as no surprise that Warhol selected Nicklaus to represent golf. "The Golden Bear" dominated the sport for nearly three decades. In total, he would win seventy-three PGA Tour events and eighteen professional majors. From the 1950s to the 1990s, only Arnold Palmer rivaled him in terms of celebrity in golf. But Warhol had little interest in what Nicklaus actually did—when asked by the artist to move his "stick" while sitting, Nicklaus shot back, "Excuse me, this is not a stick; this is a club."[40] Whether it was a club or a stick

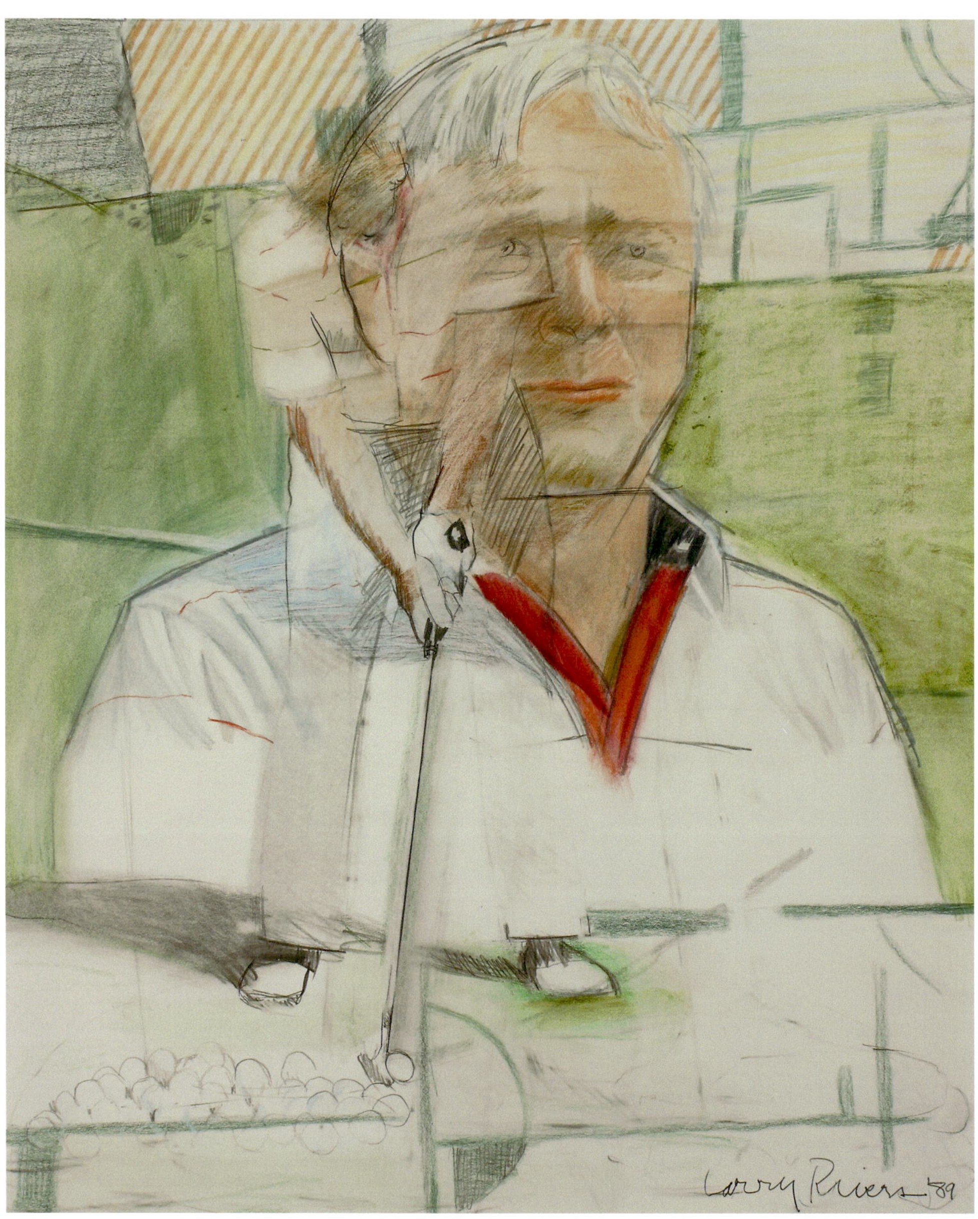

43 **LARRY RIVERS (AMERICAN, 1923–2002)**

Arnold Palmer, 1989
Colored pencil on paper, 40 × 34 inches
United States Golf Association
Museum, Far Hills, New Jersey,
courtesy USGA Museum, 1990-158

appeared to be of little interest to Warhol. What counted was Nicklaus's aura of accomplishment and fame—something the artist could craft into bold images projecting the athlete's confidence and strength.[41]

Like Warhol, Larry Rivers also expresses the conflicted relationship between American culture and values. Best known for his work *Washington Crossing the Delaware* (1953; The Museum of Modern Art, New York), Rivers trained as a jazz musician but also studied painting in New York City. He lived at the Hotel Chelsea with others associated with Warhol's Factory.[42] Warhol wrote about Rivers's influence on his own work: "Larry's painting style was unique—it wasn't Abstract Expressionism and it wasn't Pop; it fell into the period in between. But his personality was very Pop."[43]

Like Warhol, Rivers was well known for his celebrity portraits. His depiction of Arnold Palmer (plate 43) showcases one of the world's most famous golfers, who became a sporting superstar in the age of television. Palmer's bold style of play, characterized by final-round charges, drew legions of fans who called themselves "Arnie's Army."[44] In 1989, when Rivers completed this work for the collection of the USGA, Palmer was still competing (he did not retire from competitive play until 2004). The portrait was unveiled at the 1990 U.S. Senior Open. Though Palmer was in the twilight of his career, as depicted by Rivers he has a vital, modern, and approachable aura.

Through the Camera's Lens

Artists have long appreciated the technical aspect of golf and expressed a fascination with method, breaking the game down to its component parts. This is expressed in the visual inventories created by seventeenth-century Dutch artists such as Hendrick Avercamp, who depicted golfers—or *kolfers*—in characteristic attitudes set amid other forms of recreation (see plate 1). Emphasis on technique also appears in Rembrandt's *The Ringball Player* (see plate 5), a detail study seen through an open doorway, setting up a contrast between activity and idleness. Fascination with the process of the game has always been a part of the art of golf—conceived here in the fullness of both meanings. Rembrandt's illustration of the ringball player has a somewhat instructional aspect in addition to whatever moral lesson it may convey—or at least it could have been used that way by one unfamiliar with the game but wishing to play. It is easy to imagine a series of similar studies showing the player in various poses. This kind of separation of the game into discrete components would have been useful for the serious student of early golf.

In the twentieth century, photographer Harold Edgerton found a way to scientifically achieve this kind of breakdown. Inspired perhaps by the science of motion studies and

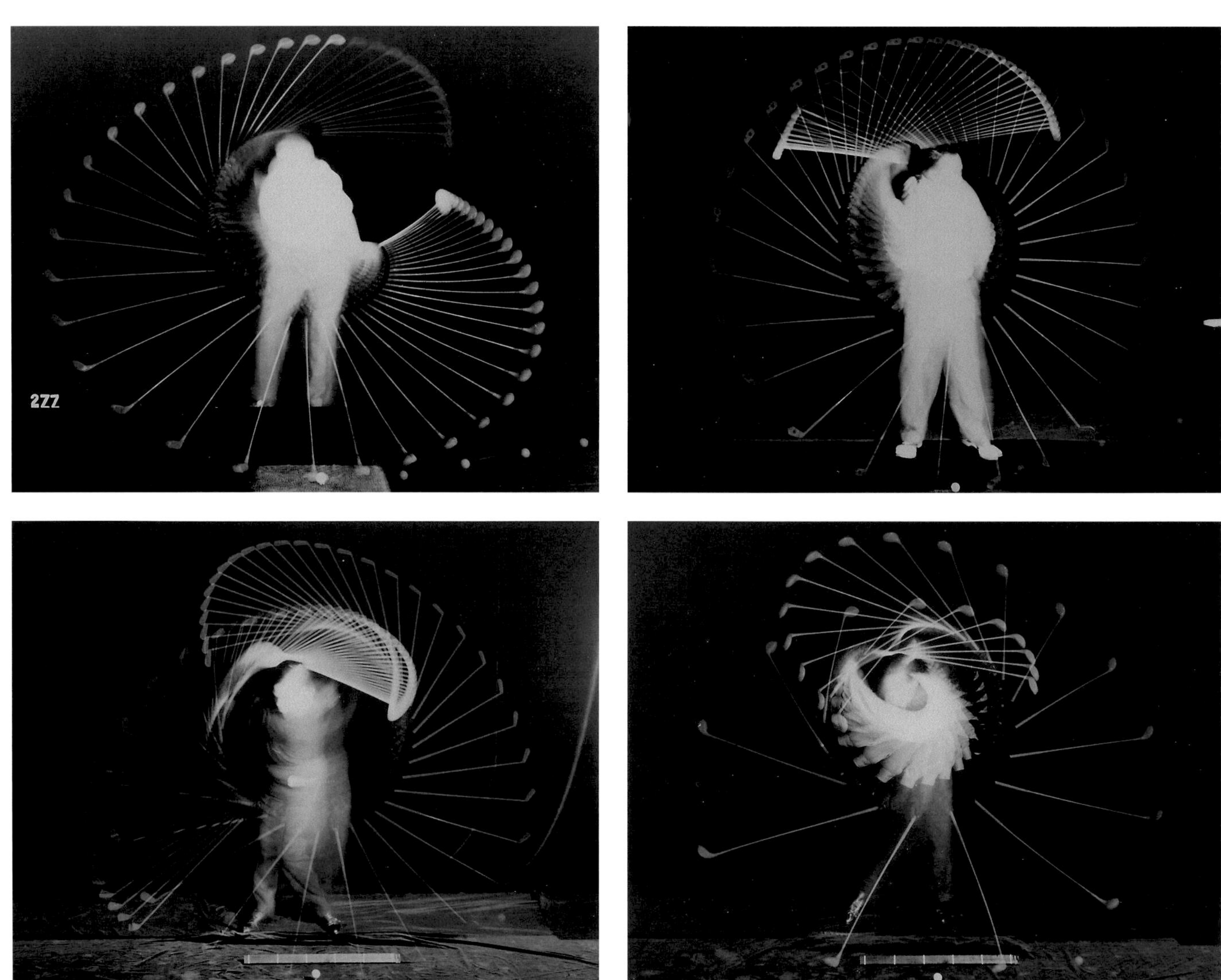

44–47 HAROLD EDGERTON (AMERICAN, 1903–1990)

Series of 16 photographs by Harold Edgerton from
Bob Jones's personal collection, 1935, printed later
Gelatin silver prints, 12 × 9 inches each (unframed)
United States Golf Association Museum, Far Hills,
New Jersey, courtesy USGA Museum, Personal Papers
of Robert T. Jones, Jr.

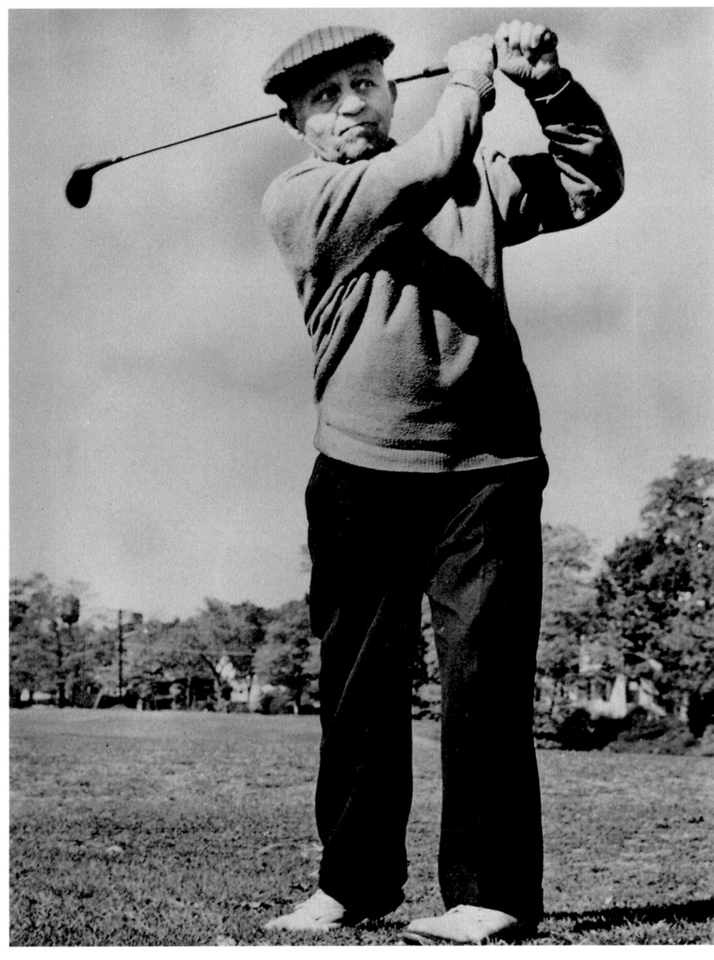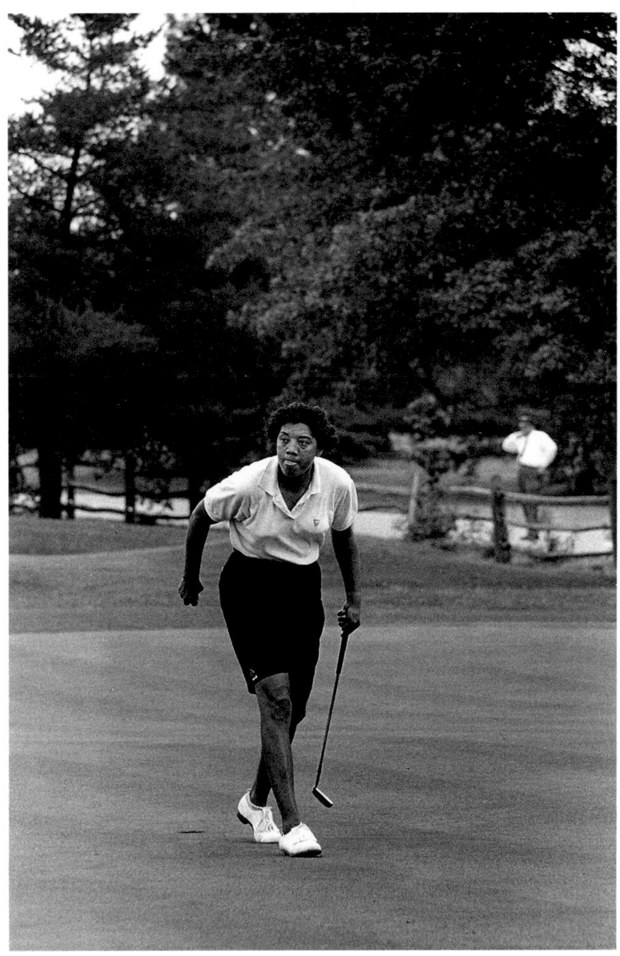

able to exploit new technologies such as stroboscopic photography, Edgerton explored the science behind golf. A native of Nebraska, Harold "Doc" Edgerton was trained at the Massachusetts Institute of Technology and joined the faculty there after completing his Ph.D.[45] He dedicated his career to photographing phenomena that are impossible to see with the naked eye or capture with traditional cameras. Edgerton's photographs of water dropping, a bullet piercing an apple, hummingbirds frozen mid-flight, children playing, or golfers in motion began appearing in both scientific journals and art exhibitions. Edgerton also developed dozens of applications for high-speed stroboscopy, including nighttime aerial photography during World War II and a method for documenting nuclear explosions. He also made important strides in both sonar and underwater photography, working with Jacques Cousteau, who called Edgerton "Papa Flash."[46] Edgerton selected Bobby Jones for a subject because of the golfer's nearly perfect swing, and he used photography to deconstruct it (plates 44–47).[47] He illustrated how the smallest nuance can have an exponential effect on the golf ball—a reality that instructors and equipment companies have long embraced. A selection of these vintage prints, donated to the USGA by the estate of Bobby Jones, is part of this exhibition.

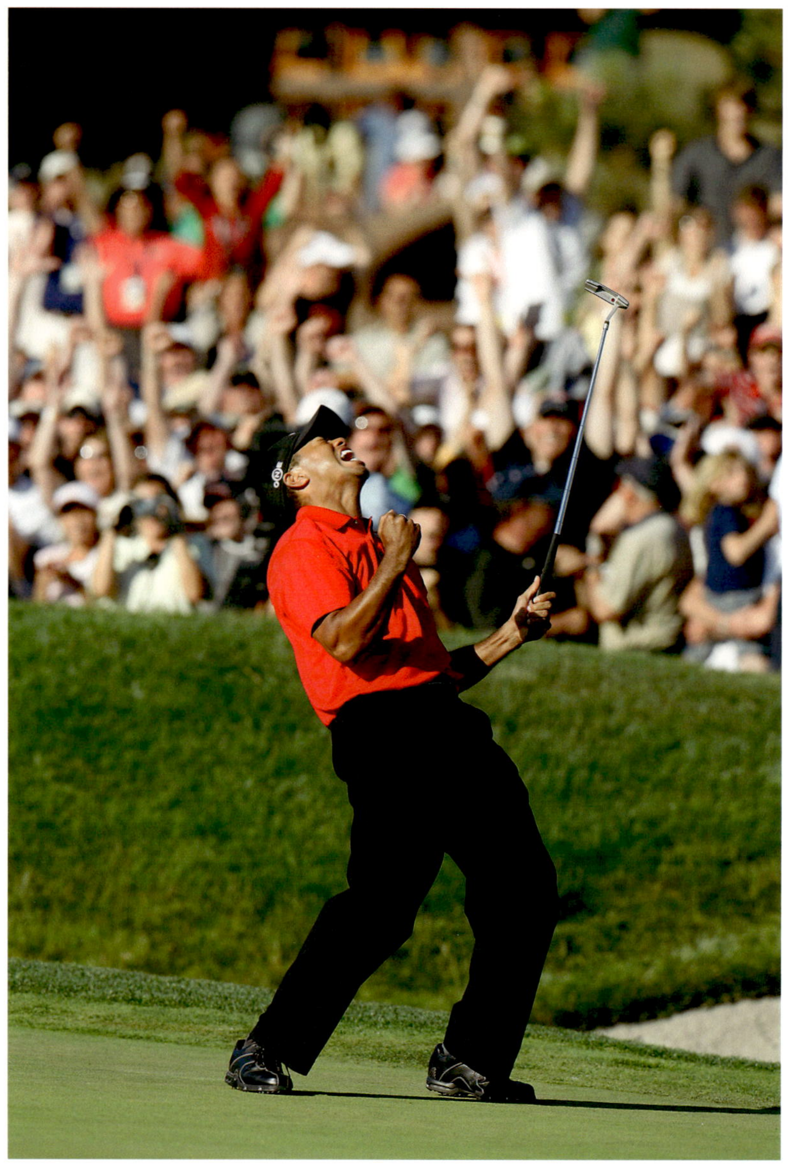

Photography also plays an important role in the social history of golf, notably document-ing the experiences of those largely excluded from the game throughout the nineteenth and early twentieth centuries. Many African American golfers were restricted from com-peting in tour events by the "Caucasians-only Clause" in effect from 1934 until 1961 in the by-laws of the Professional Golfers' Association of America.[48] They were also banned from playing at many private and public courses by either law or custom, often a combina-tion of both. The series of documentary images included in the exhibition tells the story of some of the game's legendary players. The photographs included here (plates 48–50) capture the essence of some of these courageous athletes who paved the way for contem-porary players, such as Tiger Woods. These images also show the drama and excitement of competitive play that portraits and landscapes simply cannot capture.

At its core golf is a social game that often exposes the very best, but more often the very worst, in human nature. Humor is integral to the game, and anyone who has played it knows that elements of the absurd and ridiculous are indeed "par for the course." There are thousands of jokes, cartoons, and anecdotes lambasting golf's difficulty and how it exposes a player's true character. As professional golfer Raymond Floyd once quipped, "They call it golf because all of the other four-letter words were taken"; Jack Benny reportedly said, "Give me the fresh air, a beautiful partner, and a nice round of golf, and you can keep the fresh air and the round of golf."[49] If Bobby Jones is routinely held up as the ideal sportsman, nearly everyone else who has ever played the game has had to battle for even the smallest measure of improvement. Humor, often in the form of illustrations and cartoons, helps one retain a measure of sanity in a sport that Mark Twain once called "a good walk spoiled."

Most Americans became familiar with golf and golfers in the early twentieth century through illustrations in popular magazines, many of which poked gentle fun at the increasingly popular sport. As Gary Schwartz writes in *The Art of Golf*, "What better way to appreciate the rise of golf to its eminent position in worldwide sports than by looking at the vehicles that originally represented the sport to the public: the magazine, the picture postcard, and popular advertising."[50] As Bobby Jones was gaining prominence on a national and international stage, Norman Rockwell emerged as among the nation's most recognized and respected illustrators. *Life* magazine estimated that his pictures have been seen by more people than all of Michelangelo's, Rembrandt's, and Picasso's combined.[51] Rockwell's work for the *Saturday Evening Post* was largely responsible for his widespread appeal. His style had antecedents in nineteenth-century genre painting by artists such as Eastman Johnson and William Sidney Mount, who produced vernacular art designed to appeal to middle-class

51 NORMAN ROCKWELL (AMERICAN, 1894–1978)

Old Man Tracy of Tracy and Tracy, 1926
Oil on canvas, 22 × 36 inches
United States Golf Association Museum, Far Hills,
New Jersey, courtesy USGA Museum, 1991.173

audiences. Rockwell's skill as a storyteller helped ensure that his images were accessible to the average viewer. In contrast to the more rigid Americanism advocated by artists such as Grant Wood, Rockwell's message was complex; as David Kamp wrote, "While his approach was calculatedly upbeat, it was never shallow or jingoistic, and his work, taken as a whole, is a remarkably thoughtful and multifaceted engagement with the question 'What does it mean to be an American?'"[52]

Rockwell's *Old Man Tracy of Tracy and Tracy* (plate 51) portrays the aging golfer fashionably dressed in plus fours, poring over his scorecard with a wry grin on his face. The average viewer is left to wonder at the reason for his pleasure, while golfers might secretly hope it is due to a hole in one. Rockwell created a number of illustrations devoted to golf, sympathetically focusing on the triumphs and tribulations of the game, but left serious critiques to others.

Though not included in this exhibition, other illustrators are quite significant in the history of golf, most notably A. B. Frost, whose work for *Harper's Magazine* first introduced Americans to the game. Frost trained with Thomas Eakins and William Merritt Chase and became a giant in what some call the "Golden Age of American Illustration." James Montgomery Flagg, known for his iconic illustration of Uncle Sam, was a regular contributor to *The American Golfer*, mirroring Rockwell's relationship to the *Saturday Evening Post*. In fact, most of the great illustrators of this era—Franklin Booth, Howard Chandler Christy, Harrison Fisher, Charles Dana Gibson, Arthur Ignatius Keller, Edward Penfield, and John Held, Jr.—all produced golf-themed illustrations.

Cartoonists have long used golf as a subject, parodying the game in ways that expose human foibles. One of America's most famous cartoonists, Charles Schulz, aimed his gentle humor at a middle-class audience. Schulz was an avid golfer and frequently put *Peanuts* characters Charlie Brown, Snoopy, Linus, Lucy, and others on the links. "The things I like to do the best," he said in 1967, "are drawing cartoons and hitting golf balls."[53] Born in Minneapolis, Minnesota, Schulz knew he wanted to be a cartoonist from an early age and began his career after serving in World War II. *Peanuts* was syndicated nationally in 1950, and by Schulz's retirement in 1999 the comic strip was featured in more than 2,600 newspapers and published in twenty-one languages. It remains one of the most beloved comic strips in American history. Robert C. Harvey described the strip's widespread appeal: "The achievement at the heart of *Peanuts* is the trick Schulz played with the very visual-verbal nature of his medium. The pictures show us small children. But their speech reveals that they are infected with fairly adult insecurities and quirks and other often disheartening preoccupations. The dichotomy between picture and words permits us to laugh about heartbreak."[54]

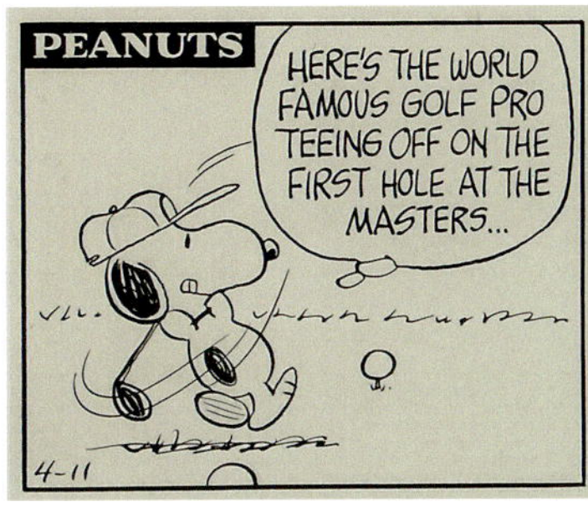

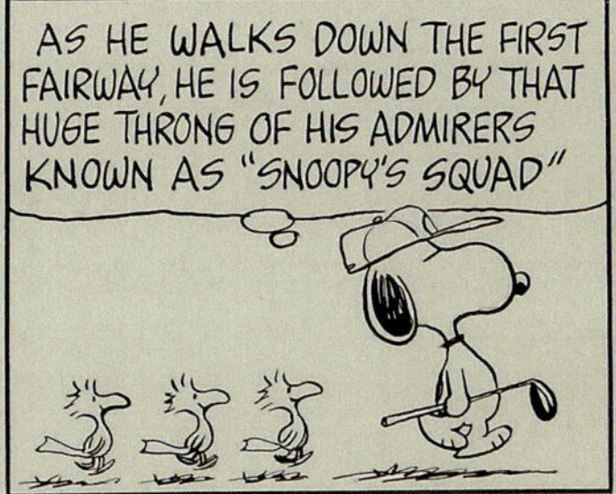

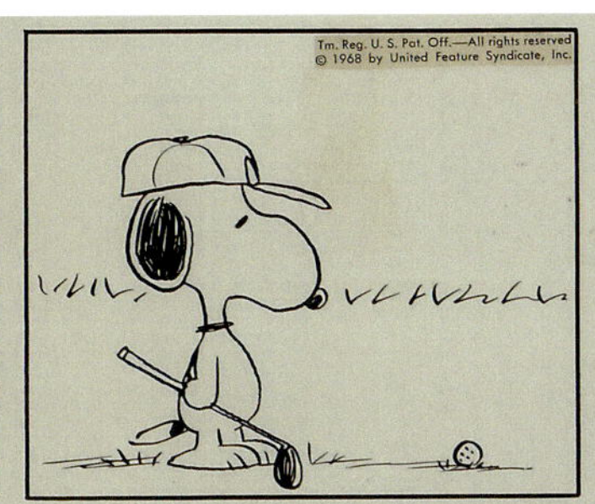

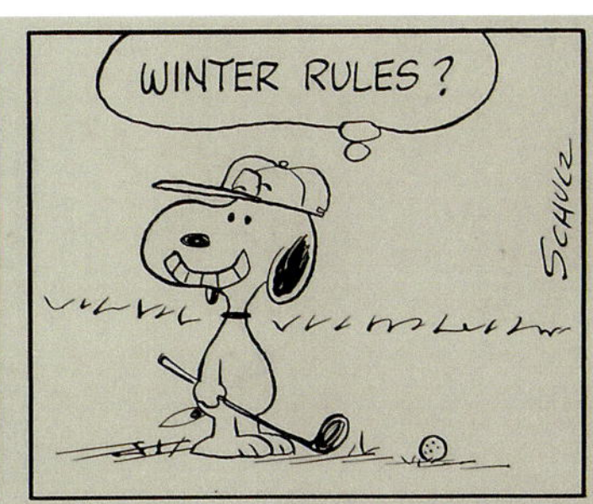

52 CHARLES SCHULZ (AMERICAN, 1922-2000)

Snoopy's Grand Slam, "World Famous Golf Pro Flies to Augusta," 1972
Ink on paper, 13 × 35 inches
United States Golf Association Museum, Far Hills, New Jersey, courtesy USGA Museum, 1973-28

The original cartoons featured in this exhibition were created for a 1972 book that Schulz created, *Snoopy's Grand Slam* (plate 52), in which Snoopy competes in the Bing Crosby Pro-Am, the Masters, and the U.S. Open. In contrast to his owner Charlie Brown, who is a chronic loser, Snoopy succeeds brilliantly at nearly every endeavor—golf is no exception.[55] These cartoons were donated by the artist to the USGA and were part of the 2010 exhibition *Snoopy on the Links* at the USGA Museum in Far Hills, New Jersey. The USGA has for many years used Snoopy in their publications, including a booklet titled *Uncle Snoopy Wants You to Know How to Use Your Handicap*. A 2000 article in *Golf Journal* declared, "It would be impossible to know how many millions could relate to the on-course failures of [Schulz's] characters; it's also impossible to estimate how many of those same people learned Equitable Stroke Control at the paws of a beagle."[56]

Though cartoons such as *Peanuts* featured and were often marketed to children, they were not exclusively intended for them. In fact, as James Billington writes in *Cartoon America*, "Cartoon art, a truly democratic art for a democratic society, has always played a special role in America. Cartoons have helped spark revolution, sway election campaigns, reveal corruption, and promote reform. They educate and entertain, inform and enlighten. Artful or awful, they are the graphic snapshots of our times, spontaneous and accessible to all."[57]

While Norman Rockwell and Charles Schulz looked to middle America, *The New Yorker* targeted the urban and sophisticated reader. The first issue of the magazine left no doubt about its audience when it published the following statement: "The purpose of *The New Yorker* will be to reflect New York life through its treatment of the lives and personalities of the day. It will not be what is called radical or highbrow. It will be what is called sophisticated . . . will publish facts which it will have to go behind the scenes to get . . . hopes to reflect metropolitan life. It will not be edited for the old lady in Dubuque."[58] First published in 1925, *The New Yorker* quickly distinguished itself as the premier magazine for serious journalism, fiction, and humor. Some of the world's best-known writers—Eudora Welty, Vladimir Nabokov, J. D. Salinger, and John Updike, among others—were featured in its pages. The magazine became famous for its cartoons, many of which used golf as a subject.

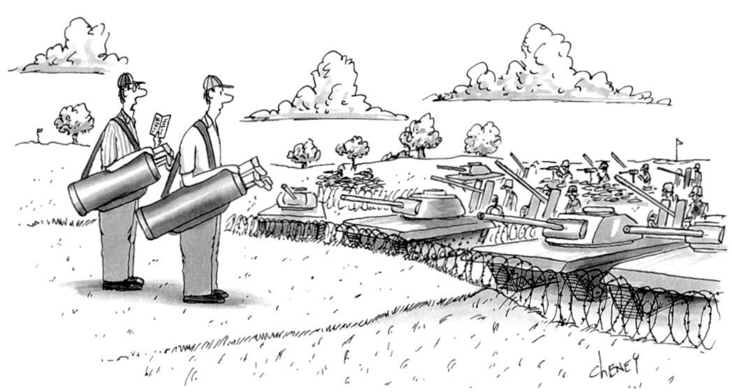

"I support our troops as much as the next guy, but do we have to let them play through?"

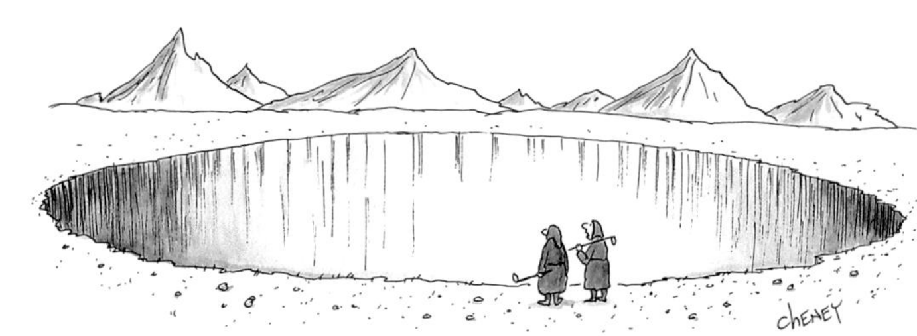

"Maybe it would be more fun with a smaller hole."

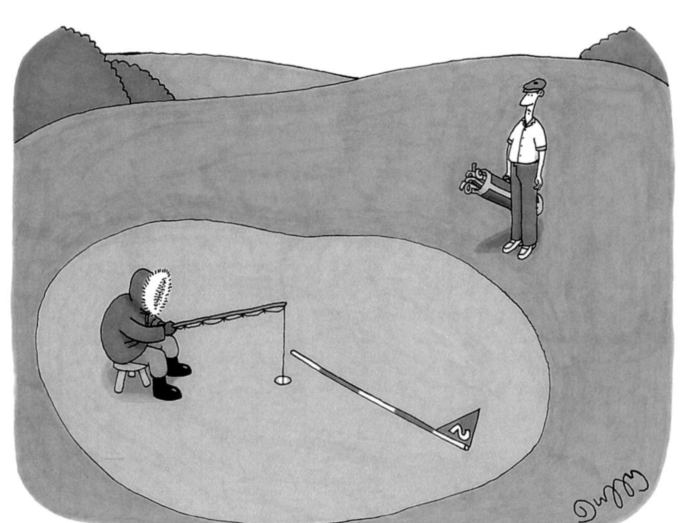

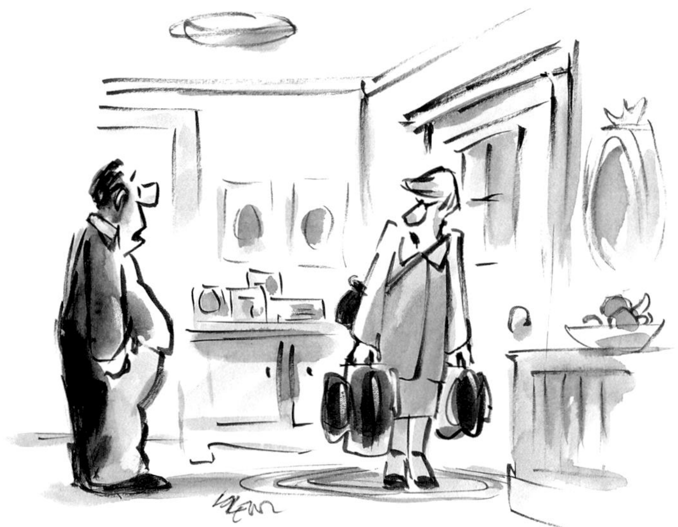

"You can't leave, Alice—you're the only thing keeping me from quitting my job, taking up golf, and living off the equity in the house."

Cartoons have been part of *The New Yorker*'s brand since its founding, and many of the most talented American humorists have showcased their work there. In the magazine's early years, the editorial staff would caption the cartoons; today the cartoonists submit the completed work for review, but it is not uncommon for them to be asked to revise it for publication.[59] In 2005 the editors began using the final page of the magazine for "*The New Yorker* Cartoon Caption Contest," inviting readers to submit captions that are then voted on by other readers.

53 TOM CHENEY (AMERICAN, BORN 1954)

"I support our troops . . . ," 2007
Ink on paper, 8½ × 11 inches
Condé Nast, *The New Yorker* Magazine,
123650

54 TOM CHENEY (AMERICAN, BORN 1954)

"Maybe it would be more fun . . . ," 2007
Ink on paper, 8½ × 11 inches
Condé Nast, *The New Yorker* Magazine,
123904

55 J. C. DUFFY (AMERICAN)

Inuit Fishing on a Golf Green, 2006
Ink on paper, 9 × 11½ inches
Condé Nast, *The New Yorker* Magazine,
122612

56 LEE LORENZ (AMERICAN, BORN 1933)

"You can't leave, Alice . . . ," 2006
Ink on paper, 14 × 17 inches
Condé Nast, *The New Yorker* Magazine,
122734

Golf has been a frequent topic for the cartoonists, and over the years they have captured the essence of the sport Winston Churchill once described as "chasing a quinine pill around a cow pasture." The three cartoonists whose work is shown here have long associations with the publication. Tom Cheney's cartoons (plates 53–54) have appeared in more than five hundred publications, including *National Lampoon* and the *Harvard Business Review*. He was given the Charles M. Schulz Outstanding Cartoonist Award in 1985 and is today a staff cartoonist for *The New Yorker*. J. C. Duffy (plate 55) is a regular contributor to *The New Yorker* but is best known as the artist of the comic strip "The Fusco Brothers," which was syndicated in 1989 and is carried by more than one hundred newspapers. Lee Lorenz (plate 56) is a noted American cartoonist whose work first appeared in *The New Yorker* in 1956. Two years later, he was a commissioned artist and worked as an art editor at the magazine from 1973 to 1998. In 1995 Lorenz was given the National Cartoonist Society Gag Cartoon Award. He has edited several books, including *The Art of The New Yorker: 1925–1995* (1995), and he authored the introduction to *The World of William Steig* (1998).[60] More than Rockwell or Schulz, whose gentle critiques of golf never cut too deeply, *The New Yorker* often put the rules of golf in collision with the rules of society in more profound ways. Underlying Cheney's *I support our troops* (see plate 53) is the very serious concern that club members and the elite are asked to make few sacrifices during wartime. Seemingly gentle cartoons elicit a laugh at one level but also convey a truthful irony.

Humorists outside the United States have also played a critical role in parodying golf, and we have included two notable examples here. Sue Macartney Snape's critically acclaimed graphic satires of idiosyncratic British social stereotypes appear regularly in *The Daily Telegraph*. The selection featured here (plates 57–59) pokes fun at the types of eccentric characters found on courses and in clubhouses in the British golf world, including the wily and embattled caddy; the pompous, tradition-obsessed veteran golfer; and the matronly lady golfer. Scottish artist, illustrator, and writer Hugh Dodd's illustrative work (plates 60–62) is featured regularly in Scottish and national press, and his caricatures satirizing golf have been reproduced in print, cards, and books.

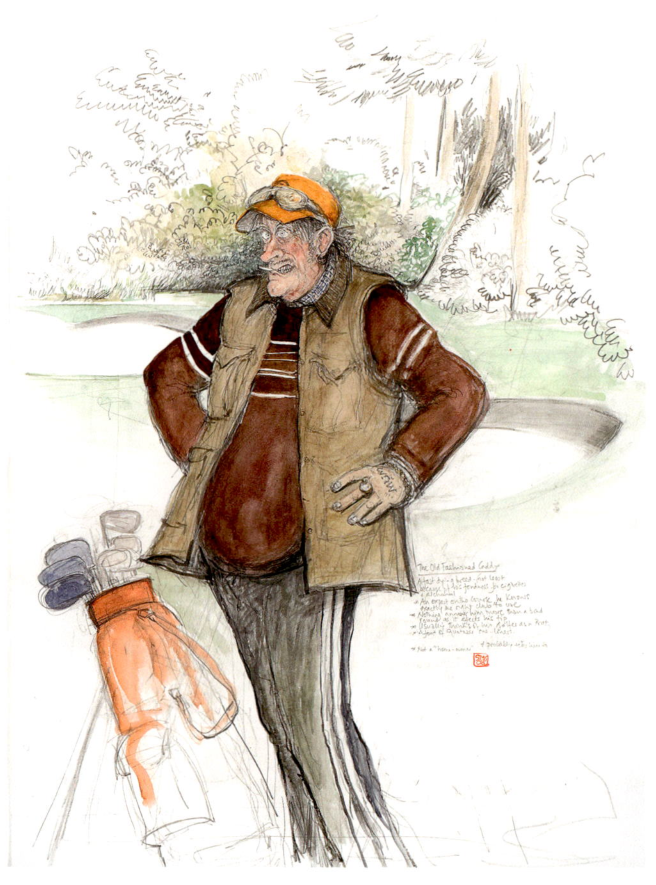

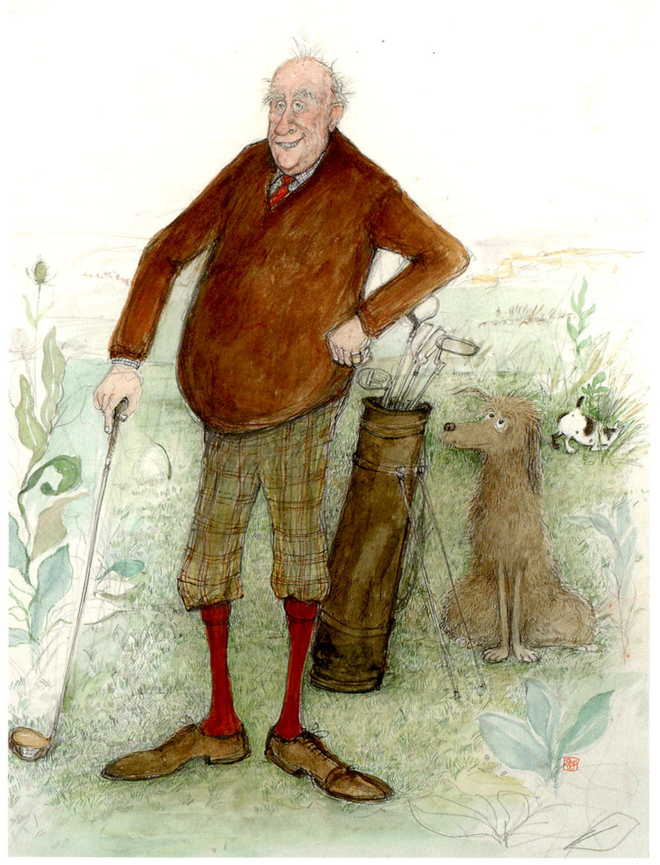

57 SUE MACARTNEY SNAPE (AUSTRALIAN, BORN TANZANIA, 1954)

The Old Fashioned Caddy, 2008
Watercolor on paper, 23 × 16 inches
Sue Macartney Snape Limited, courtesy of the artist

58 SUE MACARTNEY SNAPE (AUSTRALIAN, BORN TANZANIA, 1954)

The Golfer, 2000
Watercolor on paper, 23 × 16 inches
Sue Macartney Snape Limited, courtesy of the artist

59 SUE MACARTNEY SNAPE (AUSTRALIAN, BORN TANZANIA, 1954)

The Passionate Golfer, 2004
Watercolor on paper, 23 × 16 inches
Sue Macartney Snape Limited, courtesy of the artist

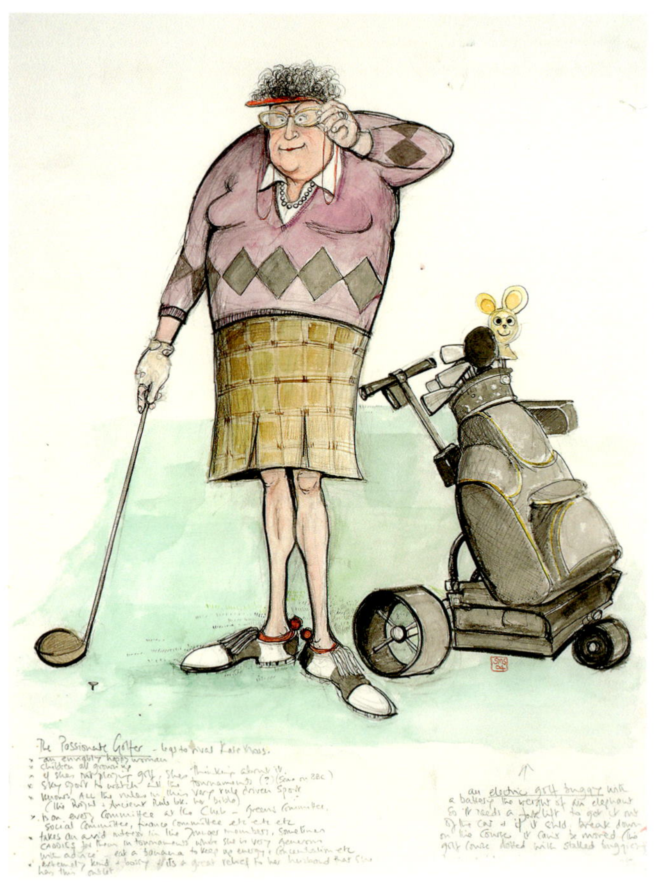

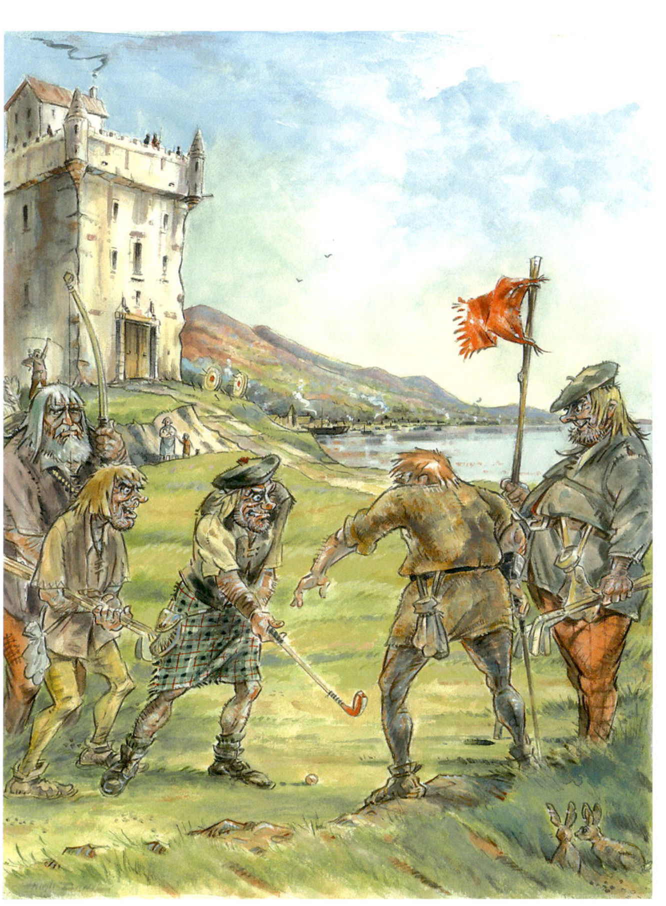

60 HUGH DODD (SCOTTISH, BORN 1948)

Early Scottish Golf: Preparing for Battle, 2010
Watercolor and gouache, 15 × 11 inches
Courtesy of the artist

61 HUGH DODD (SCOTTISH, BORN 1948)

Hickory Power Play, 2010
Watercolor and gouache, 15 × 11 inches
Collection of Lorn MacNeal

62 HUGH DODD (SCOTTISH, BORN 1948)

The Club Champion, 2010
Watercolor and gouache, 13 × 9½ inches
Courtesy of the artist

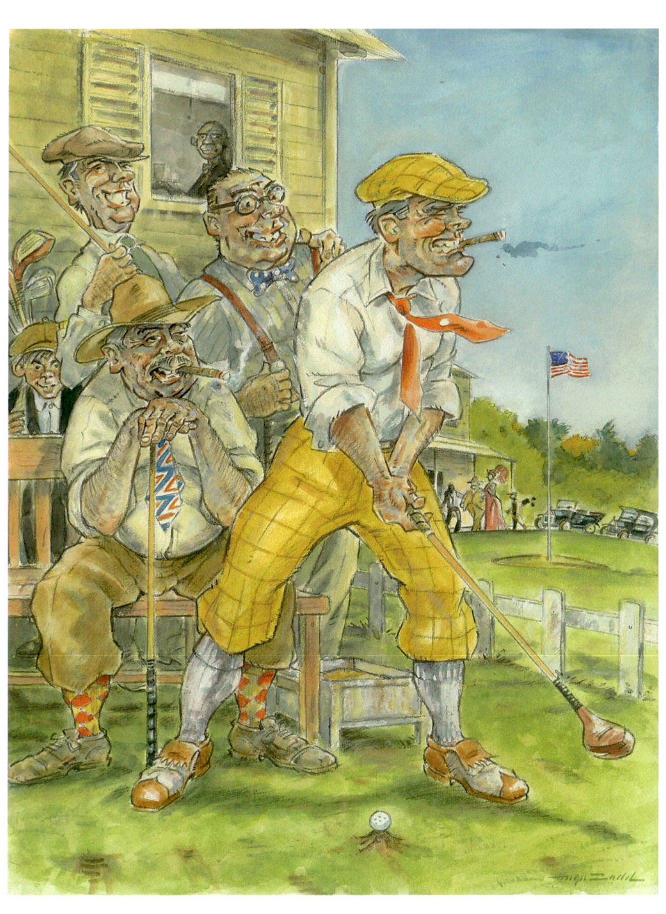

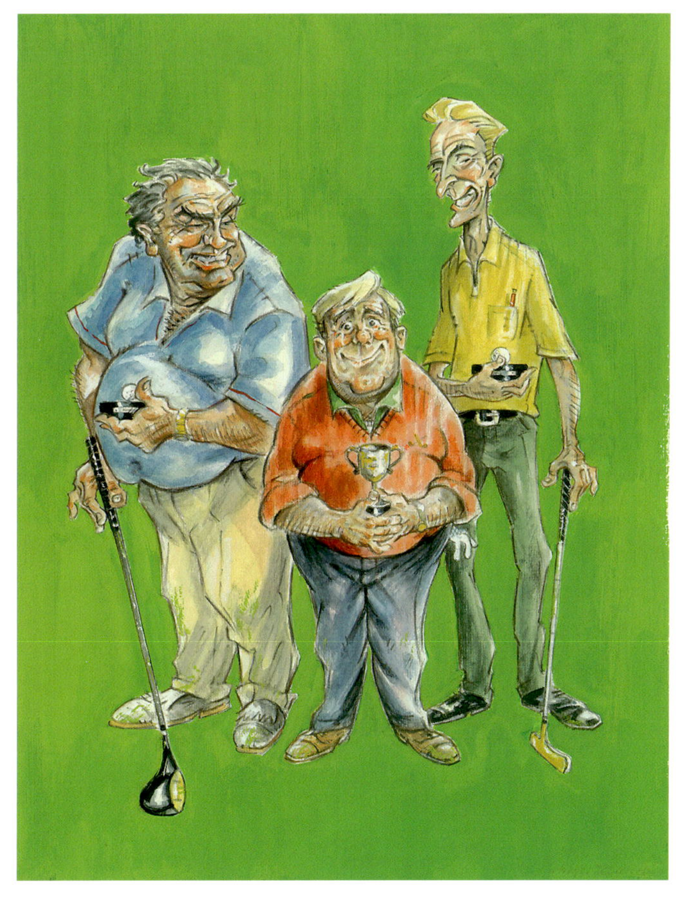

In this way, how golf is represented reflects broad transformations in the American psyche. It is not a homegrown sport like baseball or basketball; it cannot even be said to be America's game. In fact, it retains the connection to its heritage as a Scottish import now sewn into the American social fabric. Golf is emblematic of bonds of friendship across the Atlantic. There is no iconic golfing image in American art in the way that Charles Lees's grand painting *The Golfers* occupies this space in Scotland. This may well be a reflection of the game's richness and complexity. But as J. Carter Brown once said, sports such as golf help us "leave behind the toils and trouble of daily life in search of pleasure, exercise, and spirited competition."[61] This was true when George Bellows was painting in 1917, it was true when Harold Edgerton was experimenting photographically with Bobby Jones's swing in the 1930s, and it remains true today. The friendly amateur competitions of the late nineteenth century have given way to satellite television and million-dollar purses, and artists have reflected this evolution in the past century in America. The spirit of the game that grips players with what Bobby Jones called "considerable passion," however, remains unchanged.

NOTES

1 Though known by the public as "Bobby" Jones, the golfer never liked the diminutive of Robert and preferred to be known as Bob Jones. As this essay examines his public persona, the authors use Bobby throughout because it is familiar to most readers even while recognizing that this was not Jones's preference.

2 George B. Kirsch, *Golf in America* (Urbana: University of Illinois Press, 2009), 8–9.

3 Bruno Lasker, "The Psychology of Recreation," *The Survey* 46 (September 24, 1921): 711.

4 George Peper, ed., *Golf in America: The First One Hundred Years* (New York: Harry N. Abrams, 1994), 9–14. They were known as the "Apple Tree Gang" because the nineteenth hole at Saint Andrew's Golf Club was an apple tree on which members hung their coats as they enjoyed their lunches. Gary H. Schwartz, *The Art of Golf: 1754–1940* (Tiburon, CA: Wood River Publishing, 1990), 18.

5 Schwartz, *The Art of Golf*, 7.

6 Ibid., 18.

7 In 1901 golf was largely out of reach for working men and women, as annual dues at country clubs were $135, with monthly dues of $25, which did not include caddie fees or clothing and equipment. The average non-agricultural worker made about $500 per year; clerical workers, ministers, and federal employees made about $1,000. See Kirsch, *Golf in America*, 11–12, and Schwartz, *The Art of Golf*, 12.

8 See Benjamin Rader, *American Sports: From the Age of Folk Games to the Age of Televised Sports* (Upper Saddle River, NJ: Prentice Hall, 1999).

9 This could be said of other individual and team sports, including baseball, track and field, basketball, and football.

10 Golf courses from this period are consistently ranked among the top one hundred by *Golf Digest*, a ranking that began in 1966. In the 2010–2011 ranking, fourteen out of twenty courses were created before 1933. See http://www.golfdigest.com/golf-courses/2011-05/100-greatest-golf-courses. Accessed June 15, 2011.

11 Donald Holden, *Whistler Landscapes and Seascapes* (New York: Watson-Guptill Publications, 1969), 18.

12 See H. Barbara Weinberg, *Childe Hassam: American Impressionist* (New Haven: Yale University Press, 2004), 231–250.

13 Virginia Dajani, "Childe Hassam," in *Sport in Art from American Museums*, ed. Reilly Rhodes (New York: Universe, 1990), 82.

14 Weinberg, *Childe Hassam*, 246.

15 Dajani, "Childe Hassam," 82.

16 Michael Quick, Marianne Doezema, Franklin Kelly, Jane Myers, and John Wilmerding, *The Paintings of George Bellows*, ed. Nancy Stevens (New York: Harry N. Abrams, 1992), 238, quoted in Charles W. Morgan, *George Bellows: Painter of America* (New York: Reynal and Company, 1965), 37.

17 John Wilmerding, "The Art of George Bellows and the Energies of Modern America," in Quick et al., *The Paintings of George Bellows*, 2. The origin of the term "Ashcan School" has been a topic of some debate; see Donald Braider, *George Bellows and the Ashcan School of Painting* (New York: Doubleday, 1971), 91.

18 Braider, *George Bellows*, 14–15.

19 Marianne Doezema, *George Bellows and Urban America* (New Haven: Yale University Press, 1992), 6.

20 Michael Quick, "Technique and Theory: The Evolution of George Bellows's Painting Style," in Quick et al., *The Paintings of George Bellows*, 55.

21 Ibid., 63.

22 Kirsch, *Golf in America*, 15.

23 Ibid., 14.

24 See Rhonda Glenn, *An Illustrated History of Women's Golf* (Lanham, MD: Taylor Trade Publishing, 1991), and Schwartz, *The Art of Golf*, 24.

25 See http://www.artinfo.com/galleryguide/20209/6744/6233/fischbach-gallery-new-york/artist/john-falato/biography/. Accessed July 6, 2011.

26 Robin Pogrebin, "In Search of the Venus of 37th and Madison," *New York Times*, December 4, 2005. See also Naomi Yang, "John Yang Photo," http://www.johnyangphoto.com. Accessed May 10, 2011.

27 These projects eventually resulted in two books: *Over the Door: The Ornamental Stonework of New York* (Princeton: Princeton Architectural Press, 1995) and *Mount Zion: Sepulchral Portraits* (New York: Distributed Art Publishers, 2001).

28 Yang, "John Yang Photo."

29 In 1930 the Grand Slam comprised the British Amateur, the British Open, the U.S. Open, and the U.S. Amateur. Today it consists of the British Open, the U.S. Open, the Masters, and the PGA Championship.

30 For a comparison between Jones and Hagen, see Stephen Lowe's *Sir Walter and Mr. Jones: Walter Hagen, Bobby Jones, and the Rise of American Golf* (Ann Arbor: Sports Media Group, 2004).

31 Sid Matthew, *The Life and Times of Bobby Jones* (Chelsea, MI: Sleeping Bear Press, 1995), 164.

32 Ibid., 168.

33 Catherine M. Lewis, *Considerable Passions: Golf, the Masters and the Legacy of Bobby Jones* (Chicago: Triumph Books, 2000), 105–107.

34 Donald B. Goodall, "Introduction," in *Yasuo Kuniyoshi, 1889–1953: A Retrospective Exhibition*, exh. cat. (Austin: University of Texas, 1975), 9–14.

35 "Art: Sad Man," *Time,* April 13, 1948, http://www.time.com/time/magazine/article/0,9171,779802-2,00.html. Accessed May 10, 2011.

36 Goodall, "Introduction," 31–32.

37 Frayda Feldman and Jörg Schellmann, eds., *Andy Warhol Prints: A Catalogue Raisonné* (New York: Ronald Feldman Fine Arts, 1985), 10.

38 David Bourdon, *Warhol* (New York: Harry N. Abrams, 1989), 9.

39 Andy Warhol, quoted in Rainer Crone, *Andy Warhol: A Picture Show by the Artist* (New York: Rizzoli, 1987), 22.

40 Geoff Gehman, "Warhol-ized Athletes: Collector Commissioned Works to Narrow Gap Between Sports and Art," *McClatchy Tribune Business News* (Washington), September 24, 2006, 1.

41 Nicklaus Baume, "About Face," in *About Face: Andy Warhol Portraits* (Minneapolis: Print Craft, 1999), 86.

42 Larry Rivers Foundation, http://www.larryriversfoundation.org/bio.html. Accessed July 27, 2011. In sum, Palmer won seven professional majors and sixty-one PGA Tour victories.

43 Andy Warhol, *Popism: The Warhol Sixties* (New York: Harcourt Brace Jovanovich, 1980), 13.

44 Peper, ed., *Golf in America*, 261–262.

45 Gus Kayafas, ed., *Stopping Time: The Photographs of Harold Edgerton* (New York: Harry N. Abrams, 1987), 16.

46 "Harold Edgerton: Photography Pioneer," *Chicago Tribune*, January 5, 1990, 11.

47 Edgerton continued to experiment with golf, photographing a driver hitting a golf ball in 1935 and 1962, professional golfer Denny Shute hitting a ball in 1938, and a bouncing golf ball in 1951. See Kayafas, ed., *Stopping Time*.

48 Dan Levinson, Robert Fernandez, and Michael Faye, *Par* (Toronto: Blok Design, 2010).

49 Robert Winder, *The Quotable Golfer* (Philadelphia: Running Press, 1998), 167.

50 Schwartz, *The Art of Golf*, 7.

51 Donald Walton, *A Rockwell Portrait* (Kansas City: Sheed, Andrews, and McMeel, 1978).

52 David Kamp, "Norman Rockwell's American Dream," *Vanity Fair*, November 2009. http://www.vanityfair.com/culture/features/2009/11/norman-rockwell-200911. Accessed May 1, 2011.

53 David Shefter, "Snoopy Exhibit Takes Center Stage at USGA," January 28, 2010. http://www.usgamuseum.com/about_museum/news_events/news_article.aspx?newsid=90. Accessed May 8, 2011.

54 Robert C. Harvey, "Charles Schulz and Mort Walker," in Harry Katz, *Cartoon America: Comic Art in the Library of Congress* (New York: Abrams, 2006), 210.

55 Ibid., 214.

56 Shefter, "Snoopy Exhibit."

57 James H. Billington, "Foreword," in Katz, *Cartoon America*, 7.

58 The quotation has been attributed to Harold W. Ross, who along with Ralph Barton, Heywood Broun, Marc Connelly, Edna Ferber, Rea Irvin, George S. Kaufman, Alice Duer Miller, Dorothy Farker, Laurence Stallings, and Alexander Woollcott was listed in the prospectus when the first magazine appeared. "The New Yorker," *Time*, March 2, 1925, and Dale Kramer, *Ross and the New Yorker* (New York: Doubleday, 1951), 61. See also Ben Yagoda, *The New Yorker and the World It Made* (Cambridge and New York: DeCapo Press, 2001); Thomas Grant, "Mythologizing Manhattan: *The New Yorker*'s New York," *American Studies* 28, no. 1 (Spring 1987): 31–46; and Brendon Gill, *Here at the New Yorker* (Cambridge and New York: DeCapo Press, 1997).

59 Steven H. Gale, "Seventy-Five Years of *The New Yorker* Cartoons: A History," *American Periodicals* 11 (2001): 95–130.

60 Lee Lorenz, *The Art of the New Yorker* (New York: Knopf, 1995), and William Steig, *The World of William Steig* (New York: Artisan, 1998).

61 J. Carter Brown, "Introduction," in Rhodes, ed., *Sport in Art*, 82.

Checklist of the Exhibition

Paul Bril (Flemish, 1554–1626)
Landscape with Men Playing "Mail à la Chicane," 1624
Oil on canvas, 26⅝ × 34¾ inches
Minneapolis Institute of Arts, Minneapolis,
the William Hood Dunwoody Fund, 40.3
Plate 4

Aert van der Neer (Dutch, 1603–1677)
Skaters and Kolf Players on a Frozen Waterway, ca. 1630
Oil on panel, 13 × 19¼ inches
Private collection, on loan to National Galleries of
Scotland, NGL 002.96
Plate 3

Hendrick Avercamp (Dutch, 1585–1634)
Winter Landscape, ca. 1610–1620
Oil on copper, 11¼ × 16¾ inches
National Galleries of Scotland, Edinburgh, NG 647
Plate 1

Barent Avercamp (Dutch, 1612–1679)
Games on the Ice, 1654
Oil on panel, 10¾ × 17⁷⁄₁₆ inches
High Museum of Art, Atlanta, 61.8
Plate 2

Rembrandt van Rijn (Dutch, 1606–1669)
The Ringball Player, 1654
Etching on paper, 3¾ × 5¾ inches
National Galleries of Scotland, Edinburgh,
REMBRANDT.66
Plate 5

Unknown Artist
View of St Andrews from the Old Course, ca. 1740
Oil on canvas, 14 × 39⁹⁄₁₆ inches
By kind permission of The Royal and Ancient Golf Club
of St Andrews
Plate 7

William Mosman (Scottish, ca. 1700–1771)
*Sir James Macdonald (1741–1765) and Sir Alexander
Macdonald (1744–1810)*, ca. 1749
Oil on canvas, 69½ × 58 inches
National Galleries of Scotland, Edinburgh, PG 2127
Plate 8

Unknown Maker
The Silver Club, 1780s
Silver, 49⅜ inches long
By kind permission of The Royal and Ancient Golf Club
of St Andrews

David Allan (Scottish, 1744–1796)
The Prize of the Silver Golf, ca. 1785
Black ink, pencil, and watercolor on paper,
8½ × 6½ inches
National Galleries of Scotland, Edinburgh, D 387
Plate 9

David Allan (Scottish, 1744–1796)
*William Inglis (ca. 1712–1792), Surgeon and Captain of the
Honourable Company of Edinburgh Golfers*, 1787
Oil on canvas, 51 × 41½ inches
National Galleries of Scotland, Edinburgh, PG 1971
Plate 10

David Allan (Scottish, 1744–1796)
Study for *Sir William Inglis*, ca. 1787
Pen on paper, 12½ × 10½ inches
Private collection, Scotland

Unknown Artist, after David Allan
A Group of Edinburgh Characters with the Silver Golf,
ca. 1790
Pen, ink, and watercolor over pencil on paper,
7⅜ × 13½ inches
National Galleries of Scotland, Edinburgh, D 385

Sir Henry Raeburn (Scottish, 1756–1823)
*William Inglis (ca. 1712–1792), Surgeon and Captain of the
Honourable Company of Edinburgh Golfers*, ca. 1790
Oil on canvas, 55¼ × 47¾ inches
On loan to Scottish National Portrait Gallery,
Edinburgh, the Honourable Company of Edinburgh
Golfers, PGL 343
Plate 11

Sir Henry Raeburn (Scottish, 1756–1823)
John Campbell of Sadell, ca. 1815
Oil on canvas, 60¼ × 50¼ inches
The collection of John and Mary Ellen Imlay, Jr.
Plate 12

Sir Francis Grant (Scottish, 1803–1878)
Golf at North Berwick, ca. 1832–1833
Oil on canvas, 30¾ × 44¾ inches
Private collection, New York
Plate 13

Unknown Maker
Red Members' Coat, 1840s
Fabric
By kind permission of The Royal and Ancient Golf Club
of St Andrews

Unknown Maker
Feather Ball, ca. 1840s
Bull's hide and feathers
Collection of Sidney L. Matthew

Robert Adamson (Scottish, 1821–1848)
David Octavius Hill (Scottish, 1802–1870)
*St Andrews Golfers. Captain David Campbell, Allan
Robertson, Tom Morris, Bob Andrews, Sir Hugh Playfair
and Watty Alexander (Group 62)*, after 1847
Carbon print, 5¾ × 8 inches
National Galleries of Scotland, Edinburgh,
PGP HA 4750
Plate 18

Charles Lees (Scottish, 1800–1880)
Character Studies 1, 1844
Oil on paper, 22 × 11½ inches
By kind permission of The Royal and Ancient Golf Club
of St Andrews

Charles Lees (Scottish, 1800–1880)
Character Studies 2, 1844
Oil on paper, 22 × 11½ inches
By kind permission of The Royal and Ancient Golf Club
of St Andrews

Charles Lees (Scottish, 1800–1880)
Sandy Pirrie (Caddy), 1844
Oil on paper, 8½ × 7¼ inches
By kind permission of The Royal and Ancient Golf Club
of St Andrews

Charles Lees (Scottish, 1800–1880)
Sketch for *The Golfers*, 1844
Oil on millboard, 9⅛ × 12¹⁄₁₆ inches
National Galleries of Scotland, Edinburgh, PG 2019

Charles Lees (Scottish, 1800–1880)
Sketch for *The Golfers*, 1844
Oil on millboard, 14⅛ × 18⁹⁄₁₆ inches
By kind permission of The Royal and Ancient Golf Club
of St Andrews

Charles Lees (Scottish, 1800–1880)
Allan Robertson (Golf Ball Maker), ca. 1844
Oil on paper, 19¾ × 12½ inches
National Galleries of Scotland, Edinburgh, PG 2020
Plate 17

Charles Lees (Scottish, 1800–1880)
The Golfers, 1847
Oil on canvas, 51½ × 84¼ inches
National Galleries of Scotland, Edinburgh, purchased
with the assistance of the Heritage Lottery Fund,
The Art Fund, and The Royal and Ancient Golf Club of
St Andrews, 2002, PG 3299
Plate 14

Charles Lees (Scottish, 1800–1880)
Sandy Pirrie, Golfer, 1847
Oil on paper, 20 × 12³⁄₁₆ inches
National Galleries of Scotland, Edinburgh, PG 2021
Plate 16

Hugh Philip (British, 1782–1856)
Play Club, ca. 1850
Wood, leather, ram's horn, and lead, 43 inches long
United States Golf Association Museum, Far Hills,
New Jersey, courtesy USGA Museum, 1954-32

Charles Edward Wagstaffe (British, 1808–1850)
after Charles Lees
The Golfers, 1850
Stipple and line engraving on paper, 34 × 46 inches
National Galleries of Scotland, Edinburgh, SP EXL 32
Plate 15

Peter Paxton (Scottish, born 1856)
Play Club, ca. 1860
Wood, leather, ram's horn, and lead, 44 inches long
United States Golf Association Museum, Far Hills,
New Jersey, courtesy USGA Museum, 1986-28

James Good Tunny (Scottish, 1820–1887)
North British Railway Company Coach, 1865
Albumen print, 5⅞ × 8⁵⁄₁₆ inches
National Galleries of Scotland, Edinburgh, PGP 64.31

Unknown Photographer
*Lord Kyllachin, Sir Robert and Lady Finlay, Nairn Golf
Ground*, ca. 1880
Gelatin silver print, 3¼ × 3¼ inches
National Galleries of Scotland, Edinburgh, PGP 294.144

Unknown Photographer
The Ladies' Club, 1886
Photograph, 14⅛ × 22⅜ inches
British Golf Museum, St Andrews

John Charles Dollman (British, 1851–1934)
During the Time of the Sermonses, 1896
Oil on canvas, 34¹⁄₁₆ × 56¹¹⁄₁₆ inches
Harris Museum and Art Gallery, Preston,
United Kingdom
Plate 6

Unknown Photographer
*John Shippen, 1896 U.S. Open Championship,
Southampton, NY*, 1896
Gelatin silver print
United States Golf Association Museum, Far Hills,
New Jersey, courtesy USGA Museum
Plate 48

James McNeill Whistler (American, 1834–1903)
Grey and Silver: The Golf Links Dublin, 1900
Watercolor on paper, 12 × 15⅞ inches
Terra Foundation for American Art, Chicago,
Daniel J. Terra Collection, 1999.147
Plate 26

Sir George Reid (Scottish, 1841–1913)
Tom Morris, Sr., 1903
Oil on canvas, 60⅜ × 44⅜ inches
By kind permission of The Royal and Ancient Golf Club
of St Andrews
Plate 19

George Bellows (American, 1882–1925)
Golf Course, California, 1917
Oil on canvas, 30 × 38 inches
Cincinnati Art Museum, Cincinnati,
The Edwin and Virginia Irwin Memorial, 1966.6
Plate 28

Sir John Lavery (Irish, 1856–1941)
Golfing at North Berwick, ca. 1920
Oil on canvas, 32¼ × 35½ inches
The collection of John and Mary Ellen Imlay, Jr.
Plate 23

Sir John Lavery (Irish, 1856–1941)
The Golf Course, ca. 1920
Oil on canvas, 36 × 40 inches
United States Golf Association Museum, Far Hills,
New Jersey, courtesy USGA Museum, 1994-254
Plate 24

Childe Hassam (American, 1859–1935)
Dune Hazard, No. 2, 1922
Oil on canvas, 22 × 44 inches
American Academy of Arts and Letters, New York
Plate 27

Norman Rockwell (American, 1894–1978)
Old Man Tracy of Tracy and Tracy, 1926
Oil on canvas, 22 × 36 inches
United States Golf Association Museum, Far Hills,
New Jersey, courtesy USGA Museum, 1991.173
Plate 51

Wayman Adams (American, 1883–1959)
Bobby Jones, 1926
Oil on canvas, 80 × 47 inches
Courtesy Atlanta Athletic Club, John's Creek
Plate 36

Sir William Orpen (Irish, 1878–1931)
The Prince of Wales, 1927
Oil on canvas, 80 × 40 inches
By kind permission of The Royal and Ancient Golf Club
of St Andrews
Plate 20

Yasuo Kuniyoshi (American, born Japan, 1889–1953)
Self-Portrait as a Golf Player, 1927
Oil on canvas, 50¼ × 40¼ inches
The Museum of Modern Art, New York, Abby Aldrich
Rockefeller Fund, 293.1938
Plate 41

Margaret Fitzhugh Browne (American, 1884–1972)
Portrait of Bobby Jones, 1928
Oil on canvas, 37 × 31 inches
High Museum of Art, Atlanta, 28.26
Plate 37

Unknown Artist
St Andrews Welcomes You, ca. 1929
Tempera, 39 × 27 inches
Courtesy of the Cherokee Town & Country Club
Collection
Plate 21

Reginald Edward Higgins (British, 1877–1933)
Lady at St Andrews, ca. 1929
Tempera, 31 × 47 inches
Courtesy of the Cherokee Town & Country Club
Collection
Plate 22

William Steene (American, 1888–1965)
Bobby Jones, Inspired by O. B. Keeler, ca. 1930
Oil on canvas, 40 × 31½ inches
The Commerce Club, Atlanta
Plate 38

John A. A. Berrie (British, 1887–1962)
Robert T. Jones, Jr., ca. 1930
Oil on canvas, 36 × 28 inches
Courtesy of the Atlanta History Center, Atlanta
Plate 39

Unknown Artist
*Robert T. Jones Winning the British Amateur at
St Andrews*, 1930
Lithograph, 11⅛ × 16 inches
Courtesy the Yates Family
Plate 34

Harold Edgerton (American, 1903–1990)
*Series of 16 photographs by Harold Edgerton from Bob
Jones's personal collection*, 1935, printed later
Gelatin silver prints, 12 × 9 inches each (unframed)
United States Golf Association Museum, Far Hills,
New Jersey, courtesy USGA Museum, Personal Papers
of Robert T. Jones, Jr.
Plates 44–47

A. G. Spalding and Brothers
Edgerton Press Release, 1940
Ink on paper, 11 × 8 inches (unframed)
United States Golf Association Museum, Far Hills,
New Jersey, courtesy USGA Museum, Personal Papers
of Robert T. Jones, Jr.

Unknown Maker
Silver Casket, Freedom of the City of St Andrews, 1958
Silver, 4¾ × 10½ × 5¼ inches
Courtesy of the Atlanta History Center, Atlanta
Plate 35

Unknown Photographer
*Althea Gibson, 1963 U.S. Women's Open Championship,
Cincinnati, Ohio*, 1963
Gelatin silver print
United States Golf Association Museum, Far Hills,
New Jersey, courtesy USGA Museum
Plate 49

Charles Schulz (American, 1922–2000)
Snoopy's Grand Slam, "First Hole at the Masters," n.d.
Ink on paper, 13 × 35 inches
United States Golf Association Museum, Far Hills,
New Jersey, courtesy USGA Museum, 1973-28

Charles Schulz (American, 1922–2000)
Snoopy's Grand Slam, "Practice Round at the Masters,"
1972
Ink on paper, 13 × 35 inches
United States Golf Association Museum, Far Hills,
New Jersey, courtesy USGA Museum, 1973-28

Charles Schulz (American, 1922–2000)
Snoopy's Grand Slam, "Somebody Didn't Rake the Trap,"
1972
Ink on paper, 13 × 14 inches
United States Golf Association Museum, Far Hills,
New Jersey, courtesy USGA Museum, 1973-28

Charles Schulz (American, 1922–2000)
Snoopy's Grand Slam, "World Famous Golf Pro Flies to Augusta," 1972
Ink on paper, 13 × 35 inches
United States Golf Association Museum, Far Hills, New Jersey, courtesy USGA Museum, 1973-28
Plate 52

Andy Warhol (American, 1928–1987)
Jack Nicklaus, 1977
Acrylic and silkscreen ink on linen, 40 × 40 inches
The Andy Warhol Museum, Pittsburgh, Founding Collection, Contribution The Andy Warhol Foundation for the Visual Arts, Inc., 1998.1.702
Plate 42

John Yang (American, born China, 1933–2009)
Pine Valley, NJ, 1989
Gelatin silver print, 10 × 84 inches
John Yang Archive, 04.18.88-3
Plate 30

John Yang (American, born China, 1933–2009)
Merion, Ardmore, PA, 1989
Gelatin silver print, 9⅞ × 81¾ inches
John Yang Archive, 11.14.88-5
Plate 31

John Yang (American, born China, 1933–2009)
Mill River Club, Oyster Bay, NY, 1987
Gelatin silver print, 9⅞ × 85⅜ inches
John Yang Archive, 09.16.87-4
Plate 32

John Yang (American, born China, 1933–2009)
National Golf Links of America, Southampton, NY, 1989
Gelatin silver print, 9⅞ × 88¼ inches
John Yang Archive, 06.20.8-2
Plate 33

Larry Rivers (American, 1923–2002)
Arnold Palmer, 1989
Colored pencil on paper, 40 × 34 inches
United States Golf Association Museum, Far Hills, New Jersey, courtesy USGA Museum, 1990-158
Plate 43

Everett Raymond Kinstler (American, born 1926)
Bobby Jones, 1996
Oil on canvas, 42 × 56 inches
United States Golf Association Museum, Far Hills, New Jersey, courtesy USGA Museum, 1996-133
Plate 40

Sue Macartney Snape (Australian, born Tanzania, 1954)
The Golfer, 2000
Watercolor on paper, 23 × 16 inches
Sue Macartney Snape Limited, courtesy of the artist
Plate 58

Sue Macartney Snape (Australian, born Tanzania, 1954)
The Passionate Golfer, 2004
Watercolor on paper, 23 × 16 inches
Sue Macartney Snape Limited, courtesy of the artist
Plate 59

Lee Lorenz (American, born 1933)
"You can't leave, Alice . . . ," 2006
Ink on paper, 14 × 17 inches
Condé Nast, *The New Yorker* Magazine, 122734
Plate 56

John Falato (American, born 1940)
Ninth Hole, Yale University Golf Club, 2006
Oil on canvas, 8 × 16 inches
United States Golf Association Museum, Far Hills, New Jersey, courtesy USGA Museum
Plate 29

J. C. Duffy (American)
Inuit Fishing on a Golf Green, 2006
Ink on paper, 9 × 11½ inches
Condé Nast, *The New Yorker* Magazine, 122612
Plate 55

Tom Cheney (American, born 1954)
"I support our troops . . . ," 2007
Ink on paper, 8½ × 11 inches
Condé Nast, *The New Yorker* Magazine, 123650
Plate 53

Tom Cheney (American, born 1954)
"Maybe it would be more fun . . . ," 2007
Ink on paper, 8½ × 11 inches
Condé Nast, *The New Yorker* Magazine, 123904
Plate 54

Sue Macartney Snape (Australian, born Tanzania, 1954)
The Old Fashioned Caddy, 2008
Watercolor on paper, 23 × 16 inches
Sue Macartney Snape Limited, courtesy of the artist
Plate 57

John Mummert (American)
Tiger Woods, 2008 U.S. Open Championship, San Diego, California, 2008
Digital image
United States Golf Association Museum, Far Hills, New Jersey, courtesy USGA Museum/John Mummert
Plate 50

Hugh Dodd (Scottish, born 1948)
Early Scottish Golf: Preparing for Battle, 2010
Watercolor and gouache, 15 × 11 inches
Courtesy of the artist
Plate 60

Hugh Dodd (Scottish, born 1948)
Hickory Power Play, 2010
Watercolor and gouache, 15 × 11 inches
Collection of Lorn MacNeal
Plate 61

Hugh Dodd (Scottish, born 1948)
The Club Champion, 2010
Watercolor and gouache, 13 × 9½ inches
Courtesy of the artist
Plate 62

Patricia Macdonald (Scottish, born 1945) with Angus Macdonald (Scottish, born 1945)
St Andrews: "Old Course," 2011, from *Bunkered Terrain: Golf Landscapes, Scotland, 2011* (six-part work), part of the ongoing series *The Play Grounds*, 2011
Photograph, 40 × 26 inches
National Galleries of Scotland, Edinburgh, PGP 809.1

Patricia Macdonald (Scottish, born 1945) with Angus Macdonald (Scottish, born 1945)
Carnoustie: the Barry Burn and "The Island," 2011, from *Bunkered Terrain: Golf Landscapes, Scotland, 2011* (six-part work), part of the ongoing series *The Play Grounds*, 2011
Photograph, 40 × 26 inches
National Galleries of Scotland, Edinburgh, PGP 809.2

Patricia Macdonald (Scottish, born 1945) with Angus Macdonald (Scottish, born 1945)
Muirfield: the 10th, 2011, from *Bunkered Terrain: Golf Landscapes, Scotland, 2011* (six-part work), part of the ongoing series *The Play Grounds*, 2011
Photograph, 40 × 26 inches
National Galleries of Scotland, Edinburgh, PGP 809.3

Patricia Macdonald (Scottish, born 1945) with Angus Macdonald (Scottish, born 1945)
Gleneagles: "PGA Centenary Course": the 9th ("Crook o' Moss"), 2011, from *Bunkered Terrain: Golf Landscapes, Scotland, 2011* (six-part work), part of the ongoing series *The Play Grounds*, 2011
Photograph, 40 × 26 inches
National Galleries of Scotland, Edinburgh, PGP 809.4

Patricia Macdonald (Scottish, born 1945) with Angus Macdonald (Scottish, born 1945)
New course under construction, Gleneagles, 2011, from *Bunkered Terrain: Golf Landscapes, Scotland, 2011* (six-part work), part of the ongoing series *The Play Grounds*, 2011
Photograph, 40 × 26 inches
National Galleries of Scotland, Edinburgh, PGP 809.5

Patricia Macdonald (Scottish, born 1945) with Angus Macdonald (Scottish, born 1945)
Archerfield Links (the 18th, Dirleton Links Golf Course, and Clubhouse), East Lothian, 2011, from *Bunkered Terrain: Golf Landscapes, Scotland, 2011* (six-part work), part of the ongoing series *The Play Grounds*, 2011
Photograph, 40 × 26 inches
National Galleries of Scotland, Edinburgh, PGP 809.6
Plate 25

Catherine M. Lewis, Ph.D.

Dr. Catherine Lewis is a professor of history, Director of the Museum of History and Holocaust Education, and Executive Director of Museums, Archives and Rare Books at Kennesaw State University. She holds both an M.A. and Ph.D. in American studies from the University of Iowa. Lewis is the author, co-author, or co-editor of nine books, including *Considerable Passions: Golf, the Masters, and the Legacy of Bobby Jones* and *Bobby Jones and the Quest for the Grand Slam*. Lewis is also a guest curator and special projects coordinator at the Atlanta History Center, where she has curated more than twenty exhibitions, including the award-winning *Down the Fairway with Bobby Jones*.

Richard Anthony Lewis, Ph.D.

An expert on nineteenth-century American art and culture, Dr. Richard A. Lewis holds graduate degrees in art history from Northwestern University. Before joining the Louisiana State Museum in 2007, he held academic and museum positions at the National Gallery of Art, the Mariners' Museum, Towson State University, Middlebury College Museum of Art, and the University of Southern Mississippi. Lewis is author of several books and catalogues, including *Robert W. Tebbs, Photographer to Architects: Louisiana Plantations in 1926*, and has curated more than seventy-five exhibitions at a dozen institutions, including two forthcoming at the Louisiana State Museum: *The Louisiana Plantation Photographs of Robert Tebbs* (December 2011) and *First Steamboat on Western Rivers: The Legacy of New Orleans, 1811–1812* (January 2012).

Rand Jerris, Ph.D.

Dr. Rand Jerris currently serves the United States Golf Association as its Senior Managing Director of Public Services, though he has been with the USGA in various capacities since 1988. Jerris received his master's degree from Williams College in 1994 and his Ph.D. in art and archaeology from Princeton University in 1999. As Director of the USGA Museum from 2002 to 2011, Jerris oversaw the collections of historical materials housed at the USGA's headquarters in Far Hills, New Jersey. Jerris has authored three books on golf: *Golf's Golden Age: Robert T. Jones, Jr., and the Legendary Players of the '10s, '20s, and '30s*, *The Game of Golf and the Printed Word: 1566–2005* (with Richard E. Donovan), and *The Historical Dictionary of Golf* (with Bill Mallon).

Jordan Mearns   Jordan Mearns is a research assistant at the Scottish National Gallery and a Ph.D. candidate at the University of Edinburgh. His academic interests lie in eighteenth-century British visual culture and have recently been focused on the Scottish portrait painter Sir Henry Raeburn. Mearns's doctoral thesis will examine the critical reception of works by Scottish artists and artists exhibiting Scottish scenes in London in the late eighteenth and early nineteenth centuries.

Christian Tico Seifert, Ph.D.   Dr. Christian Tico Seifert studied art history, medieval history, and classical archaeology. He received his Ph.D. from the Freie Universität Berlin, where he has taught art history since 2003. He was appointed Senior Curator of Northern European Art at the National Gallery of Scotland in 2008. He has written on Italian, Netherlandish, and German art and has recently published a monograph on Pieter Lastman, Rembrandt's teacher. Dr. Seifert has organized many exhibitions, including *Dutch Mannerism* (2008) and *Dürer's Fame* (2011), and he is currently preparing a catalogue of the Dutch paintings in the collection of the National Gallery of Scotland.

PLATES

Plates 1, 5, 9: National Gallery of Scotland
Plates 2, 37: High Museum of Art, Atlanta
Plate 3: Courtesy National Galleries of Scotland
Plate 4: Courtesy of the Minneapolis Institute of Arts
Plates 6, 28: The Bridgeman Art Library
Plates 7, 19, 20: Reproduced by kind permission of The Royal and Ancient Golf Club
of St Andrews
Plates 8, 10, 11, 15–18: Scottish National Portrait Gallery
Plates 12, 23: Photo by John McKenzie
Plates 13, 21, 22, 24, 29, 38, 40, 44-47: Photo by Mike Jensen
Plate 14: Scottish National Portrait Gallery; photo by A. Reeve
Plate 25: © Patricia & Angus Macdonald/Aerographica
Plate 26: Terra Foundation for American Art, Chicago/Art Resource, New York
Plate 27: Courtesy of The American Academy of Arts and Letters, New York
Plates 30-33: © Estate of John Yang; photo by Mike Jensen
Plates 34, 35, 39: Courtesy of the Atlanta History Center
Plate 36: Courtesy of Atlanta Athletic Club
Plate 41: Art © Estate of Yasuo Kuniyoshi/Licensed by VAGA, New York. Digital image:
The Museum of Modern Art/Licensed by SCALA/Art Resource, New York
Plate 42: © 2012 Andy Warhol Foundation for the Visual Arts/Artists Rights Society
(ARS), New York. Digital image: courtesy of the Andy Warhol Museum, Pittsburgh
Plate 43: © Estate of Larry Rivers/Licensed by VAGA, New York. Photo by Mike Jensen
Plate 51: © Reproduced by courtesy of the Norman Rockwell Family Agency, Inc.
Plate 52: PEANUTS © Peanuts Worldwide LLC. Dist. By UNIVERSAL UCLICK. Reprinted
with permission. All rights reserved; photo by Mike Jensen
Plates 53-56: *The New Yorker* Magazine
Plates 57-59: Courtesy of the artist/Sue Macartney Snape Limited
Plates 60-62: Courtesy of the artist

FIGURE ILLUSTRATIONS

Fig. 1: © The Metropolitan Museum of Art/Art Resource, New York
Fig. 2: Six Art Promotion BV, Amsterdam
Fig. 3: © The Trustees of the British Museum/Art Resource, New York
Fig. 4: Courtesy of Noortman Master Paintings, Amsterdam

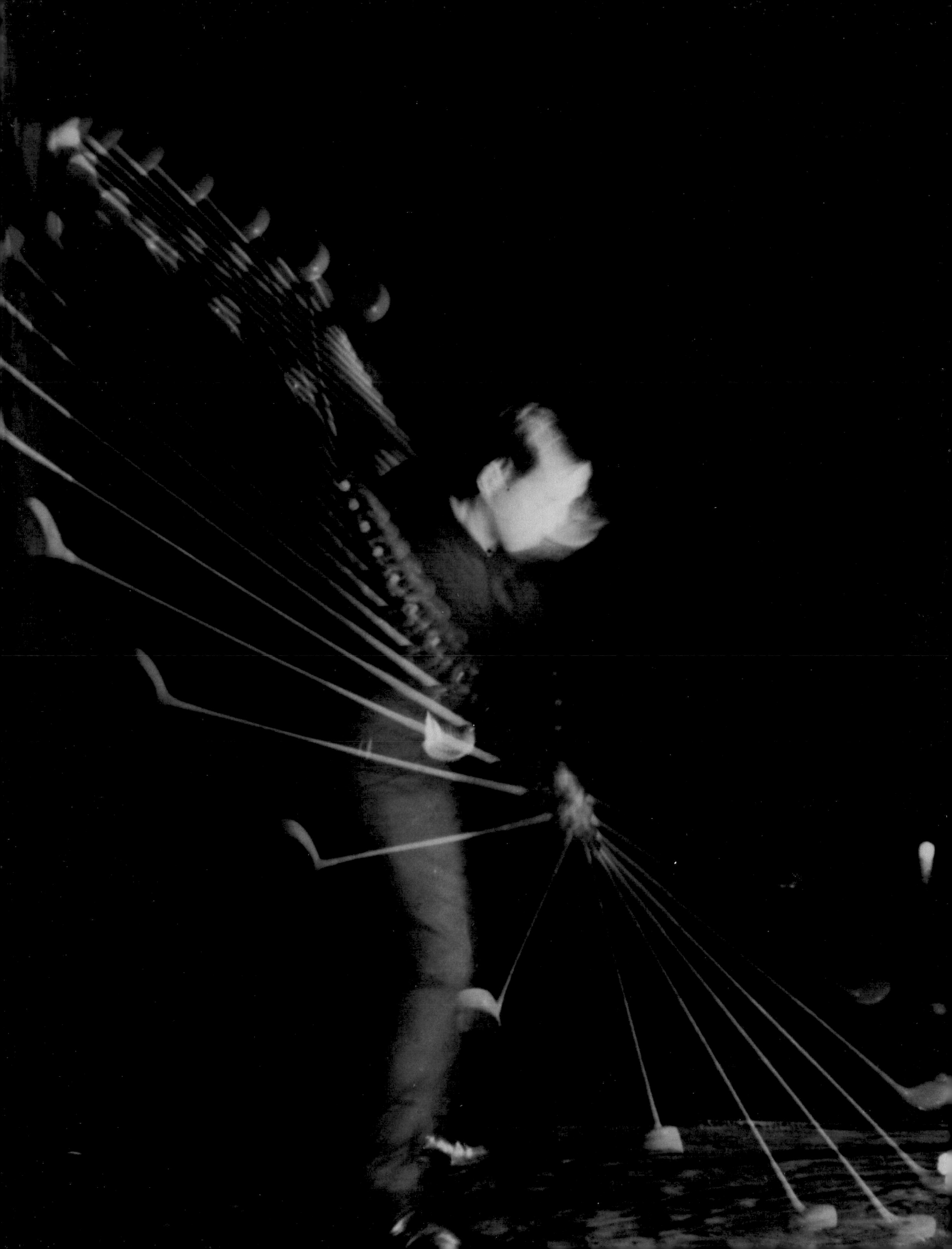

The Art of Golf is organized by the High Museum of Art, Atlanta,
in collaboration with the National Galleries of Scotland.

The exhibition is made possible by Lead Sponsor Sotheby's, The Imlay Foundation,
The Sara Giles Moore Foundation, and the Friends of Scotland: Frances Bunzl, Marcia
and John Donnell, Gayle Kennedy, Jo Ann and Nick Nicholson, Kathy and Bill Rayner,
Sharon and Chip Shirley, Margaretta Taylor, Joan N. Whitcomb, and the Dorothy and
Charlie Yates Family Fund. Additional support is provided by The Eleanor McDonald
Storza Exhibition Endowment Fund, Audio Visual Sponsor AVYVE, Alston & Bird,
Ernst & Young, King & Spalding, Norfolk Southern, Doug Hertz, and William A.
Parker, Jr.

Published on the occasion of the exhibition
The Art of Golf

High Museum of Art
Atlanta, Georgia
February 5–June 3, 2012

Library of Congress Cataloging-in-Publication Data
    The art of golf /essays by Rand Jerris, Ph.D., Catherine M. Lewis, Ph.D., Richard
Anthony Lewis, Ph.D., Jordan Mearns, Christian Tico Seifert, Ph.D.
      pages cm
    Published on the occasion of the exhibition The Art of Golf, High Museum of
Art, Atlanta, Georgia, February 5/June 3, 2012.
    The Art of Golf is organized by the High Museum of Art, Atlanta, in
collaboration with the National Galleries of Scotland.
    Includes bibliographical references.
    ISBN 978-1-932543-44-5 (alk. paper)
    1. Golf in art—Exhibitions. I. Jerris, Randon Matthew Newman, 1969– II. Lewis,
Catherine M. III. Lewis, Richard Anthony, 1963– IV. Mearns, Jordan. V. Seifert,
Christian Tico. VI. High Museum of Art. VII. National Galleries of Scotland.
    N8217.G65A78 2012
    704.9'49796352074758231—dc23   2011048819

Angela Jaeger, Senior Manager of Creative Services
Heather Medlock, Print Production Coordinator
Rachel Bohan, Associate Editor
Ewan Green, Graphic Designer

Published by the High Museum of Art, Atlanta,
in association with the University of Georgia Press

Edited by Rachel Bohan and Heather Medlock
Designed and typeset by Susan E. Kelly
Proofread by Carrie Wicks
Color management by iocolor, Seattle
Produced by Marquand Books, Inc., Seattle
Printed and bound by in China by Shenzhen Artron Color Printing Co., Ltd.